Performance and Public Value in the 'Hollow State'

SUCCESSFUL PUBLIC GOVERNANCE

**Series Editors:** Paul 't Hart, *Professor, Utrecht School of Governance, Utrecht University, the Netherlands* and Tina Nabatchi, *Director, Program for the Advancement of Research on Conflict & Collaboration, Joseph A. Strasser Endowed Professor in Public Administration, Department of Public Administration and International Affairs, Maxwell School of Citizenship and Public Affairs, Syracuse University, USA*

Societies have the best shot at thriving when they are governed through public institutions that are trustworthy, reliable, impartial, and competent. Yet in the first decades of the 21st century, governments and public institutions worldwide have been challenged by deep and fast changes in their operating environments. Thus, there is an urgent need for concepts, designs, and practices for successful public governance, which this groundbreaking new book series will seek to present.

Under the direction of the Series Editors, the series will present a number of approaches to the topic of successful public governance, including:

- *Conceptualizations* and critiques of the notion and ideal of 'success' in public sector and political settings;
- *Methodological strategies* for designing and conducting 'positive' evaluations of public policies, organisations, networks, initiatives, and other forms of public governance;
- *Empirical studies* that provide close-up, comparative, experimental, and large-n/big data research identifying, describing, explaining, and/or interpreting highly effective, highly adaptive, highly democratic, highly reputed, highly resilient public governance institutions and practices;
- *Pleas, proposals, designs* giving ideational accounts of 'what should and might be' when it comes to successful public governance.

Titles in the series include:

Pragmatism and Political Crisis Management
Principle and Practical Rationality During the Financial Crisis
*Christopher Ansell and Martin Bartenberger*

Performance and Public Value in the 'Hollow State'
Assessing Government–Nonprofit Partnerships
*Kelly LeRoux and Nathaniel S. Wright*

# Performance and Public Value in the 'Hollow State'

## Assessing Government–Nonprofit Partnerships

Kelly LeRoux

*Professor of Public Administration, College of Urban Planning and Public Affairs, University of Illinois Chicago, USA*

Nathaniel S. Wright

*Assistant Professor of Public Administration, Department of Political Science, Texas Tech University, USA*

Edward **Elgar**
PUBLISHING

Cheltenham, UK • Northampton, MA, USA

Published by
Edward Elgar Publishing Limited
The Lypiatts
15 Lansdown Road
Cheltenham
Glos GL50 2JA
UK

Edward Elgar Publishing, Inc.
William Pratt House
9 Dewey Court
Northampton
Massachusetts 01060
USA

A catalogue record for this book
is available from the British Library

Library of Congress Control Number: 2021947600

This book is available electronically in the **Elgar**online
Political Science and Public Policy subject collection
http://dx.doi.org/10.4337/9781802200393

ISBN 978 1 80220 038 6 (cased)
ISBN 978 1 80220 039 3 (eBook)

Printed and bound by CPI Group (UK) Ltd, Croydon, CR0 4YY

*To Mariel and Joe who continually inspire me for better performance – K.L.*

*To Elizabeth, Chante, and Paris, for everything that you have done for me, with all my heart I appreciate you and honor you – N.S.W.*

# Contents

| | | |
|---|---|---|
| *List of tables* | | viii |
| *About the editors and contributors* | | ix |
| *Preface and acknowledgements* | | xi |

1    Assessing performance and public value in the hollow state    1
     *Kelly LeRoux and Nathaniel S. Wright*

2    The challenge of nonprofit accountability and quality
     control in the urban hollow state: the case of public education    25
     *Michael R. Ford*

3    Are outsourced public health services linked to better
     health outcomes? Findings from a national study of service
     contracting by local health departments    43
     *Tianshu Zhao and Kelly LeRoux*

4    The role of community action agencies in facilitating
     successful sustainable development in American cities    64
     *Nathaniel S. Wright and Tony G. Reames*

5    Bridging charitable support and public service
     performance: a preliminary analysis of large US city park systems    85
     *Yuan (Daniel) Cheng, Yu Shi, and Simon A. Andrew*

6    Negotiating performance: the strategic responses of
     associations where people in poverty raise their voice    102
     *Peter Raeymaeckers and Pieter Cools*

7    Reconceptualizing performance: filling the hollow state
     with public value    125
     *Kelly LeRoux and Nathaniel S. Wright*

*Index*    *140*

# Tables

| 2.1 | Summary statistics for continuous variables | 34 |
|---|---|---|
| 2.2 | Summary statistics for categorical variables | 35 |
| 2.3 | Survival analysis predicting school closure | 36 |
| 2.4 | Multinomial logit predicting school closure | 37 |
| 3.1 | Average asset specificity and service measurability ratings | 51 |
| 3.2 | Examples of public health services with lower and higher transaction costs | 53 |
| 3.3 | Descriptive statistics | 55 |
| 3.4 | Relationship between contracting out for public health services and health outcomes for those services | 57 |
| 4.1 | Descriptive statistics and variable measures | 74 |
| 4.2 | Impact of nonprofit (CAA) organizational factors on community sustainability performance | 76 |
| 5.1 | Variable descriptions and data sources | 93 |
| 5.2 | Descriptive statistics for model variables | 94 |
| 5.3 | Impact of park-supporting charities on three measures of park system performance | 96 |
| 6.1 | Semi-structured interviews with professionals | 109 |
| 6.2 | Focus groups with APRV participants and social workers | 110 |
| 6.3 | Observation during meetings and events | 111 |
| 7.1 | A holistic approach to evaluating performance: outcomes achieved + public value creation | 128 |

# About the editors and contributors

## EDITORS

**Kelly LeRoux** is a professor in the Department of Public Administration in the College of Urban Planning and Public Affairs at University of Illinois at Chicago, USA, where she teaches courses in public policy and public and nonprofit management. Before beginning an academic career, she worked for over a decade in a nonprofit behavioral health and housing organization funded entirely by government. Her research focuses on local public service delivery, nonprofits' political activities, and issues of nonprofit performance and accountability. She is the co-author of *Nonprofit Organizations and Civil Society in the United States,* with Mary K. Feeney, and *Service Contracting, A Local Government Guide,* by ICMA Press.

**Nathaniel S. Wright** is a native of Jamaica, Queens, USA, and an emerging scholar in nonprofit management and urban policy specialized in nonprofit performance and accountability with a focus on the role that community-based nonprofits play in revitalizing urban neighborhoods. Dr Wright received his BA and Master of Public Administration from Binghamton University (2005, 2006); and PhD in Public Administration from the University of Kansas, USA (2014). He is currently an assistant professor in the Department of Political Science at Texas Tech University, USA, where he teaches courses on philanthropy and nonprofit management.

## CONTRIBUTORS

**Simon A. Andrew** is a professor in the College of Health and Public Service at the University of North Texas, USA. His work focuses on local governance, intergovernmental and interorganizational service collaboration, and policy network analysis.

**Yuan (Daniel) Cheng** is an assistant professor in the Humphrey School of Public Affairs at the University of Minnesota, USA, where he teaches public and nonprofit management. His research focuses on a range of theoretical and managerial questions lying at the nexus of governance, government–nonprofit relationships, co-production, and the distributional and performance implications of cross-sectoral collaboration, often with a substantive focus on urban sustainability.

**Pieter Cools** is professor at the Masters of Social Work at the University of Antwerp in Belgium. He wrote his PhD on social innovation and welfare reform in Belgium and England. His current research focusses on state–civil society relations and theory-driven evaluation.

**Michael R. Ford** teaches in the Masters of Public Administration program at the University of Wisconsin Oshkosh, USA. Prior to joining academia Michael worked for eight years in the nonprofit sector. His areas of research interest are public and nonprofit board governance, public sector accountability, public finance, and school choice.

**Peter Raeymaeckers** is professor at the Master of Social Work at the University of Antwerp, Belgium, and affiliated with the Center for research on Ecological and Social Change. His main topics of interest are social work evaluation research, network governance, and advocacy.

**Tony G. Reames** is an assistant professor at the University of Michigan School for Environment and Sustainability, USA, and directs the Urban Energy Justice Lab. He conducts research in the emerging field of energy justice, investigating fair and equitable access to affordable, reliable, efficient, and clean energy, and seeks to understand the production and persistence of spatial, racial, and socioeconomic residential energy disparities. He has a PhD in Public Administration from the University of Kansas, USA; a Masters in Engineering Management from Kansas State University, USA; and a Bachelor of Science in Civil Engineering from North Carolina Agricultural and Technical State University, USA. Dr Reames is also a licensed professional engineer and US Army Officer veteran.

**Yu Shi** is an assistant professor in the College of Health and Public Service at the University of North Texas, USA. Her research focuses on intergovernmental relations, public debt management, and the impact of fiscal federalism on government performance.

**Tianshu Zhao** is an assistant professor in the Graduate Center for Public Policy and Administration at California State University Long Beach, USA. Her current research focuses on public and nonprofit management, health policy, government contracting, and multi-sector collaboration.

# Preface and acknowledgements

This book emerged from our shared interest and past collaborative work on nonprofit performance that began nearly 15 years ago. Having done research on this subject together, individually, and with other co-authors, we grew to understand that this literature is highly fragmented, framed by different types of questions, and often points to inconsistent findings. Scholars of nonprofit studies often view performance questions in terms of impact, while those working from the public management perspective approach nonprofit performance through the lens of accountability. These varying frames make it difficult to arrive at a shared or cumulative understanding of nonprofit performance, particularly from vantage point of government actors who rely heavily on the nonprofit sector to deliver public services. Across the vast literature on this topic, one of most elusive questions is whether hollowing out the state and relying on nonprofits as service delivery partners has yielded positive benefits for service users, citizens, or the public more broadly. We knew that finding the answer to this question was too big a task for one person alone, and that to get at it in the way we wanted, we needed to draw on the expertise of other scholars concerned with the performance implications of government–nonprofit partnerships. While this book does not serve as the definitive word on this subject, we do hope it provides the start for a new dialogue about the ways we conceive of, and measure, performance in these service delivery partnerships.

Like any major project, the successful conclusion of this one depended on a lot of people. We would like to thank Dennis Patterson, former Chair of the Department of Political Science at Texas Tech University who planted the seed for this project during Kelly's visit to the campus in spring 2017. He challenged us to think big, and we are immensely grateful to him and the Department for their support with various aspects of this project. We are also thankful for the Department of Public Administration at the University of Illinois at Chicago (UIC) for providing graduate assistant support for this project. As our ideas around this topic began to cohere, we bounced ideas off many helpful colleagues. While too numerous to identify individually, we are especially thankful to many members of the Association for Research on Nonprofit Organizations and Voluntary Action (ARNOVA) community for providing critical feedback on both the component parts of this book as well as the whole.

We would also like to thank each of the contributors to this book, not only for the privilege of allowing us to place their work in this volume, but also for their patience and willingness to stick with us through the long trajectory of this project. Their research contributions represent the perfect constellation to showcase the variety of policy instruments involved in government–nonprofit relationships, as well as the policy arenas they span. We are excited by the great work of these talented scholars and look forward to seeing more contributions from each of them in the future.

We also deeply indebted to the series editors, Tina Nabatchi and Paul 't Hart, who were instrumental in shaping this project and helping us navigate each step of the publication process. We are especially thankful to them for pushing us at the stage of our initial proposal review, to think bigger and consider how our understanding of nonprofit performance connects to the public values literature. The work on public values, and particularly the work related to nonprofits and governance cited throughout the first and final chapters of this volume, provided somewhat of an epiphany for us, and significantly helped us develop and refine our ideas. To say this book was improved by Tina and Paul's insight is an understatement. We are truly grateful that they saw the value in this work and helped us nurture it into something much better.

Carrying a book over the finish line during a pandemic was no easy task. We are grateful to the anonymous external reviewers who gave their time during this unprecedentedly challenging year to evaluate our proposal, read draft chapters, and ultimately see the merit in this book. We are both extraordinarily thankful to our spouses and families for their support and understanding, and space to work on this project. School closures and lack of normal routines have been a source of hardship for many working parents over the past year. On this note, Kelly offers personal thanks to Adam and Kelly Nirenberg for opening their home for remote schooling, and especially Adam for providing pod leadership, tutoring, tech support, soccer instruction, and an all-around child care safety net in this most difficult year. We are beyond grateful.

# 1. Assessing performance and public value in the hollow state

## Kelly LeRoux and Nathaniel S. Wright

More than 25 years have elapsed since Milward and Provan (1993) introduced the term "hollow state" into the lexicon of public administration. These authors describe the hollow state as a metaphor for "the increasing use of third parties, often nonprofits, to deliver social services and act in the name of the state" (Milward and Provan, 2000, p. 359). While the process of government's hollowing out began decades earlier with unprecedented increases in United States (US) federal spending for health and human services in the 1960s, it accelerated throughout the 1980s and 1990s as policymakers embraced new public management (NPM) reforms emphasizing devolution, decentralization, and privatization. Indeed, the number of nonprofits in the US roughly doubled every decade between 1960 and 2000, a trend that is largely attributed to the increased availability of government funding to support these organizations (Salamon, 1995).

Thus, by the time Milward and Provan coined the term "hollow state" to describe the diminished role of government in delivering public services and the ubiquitous reliance on nonprofits for this purpose, the phenomenon had already been well established.[1] As the discipline's leading scholars began to take an academic interest in this reality and contemplate its consequences for public management, similar terms and concepts made their way into the discourse of the field, including governance (Frederickson, 1999; Lynn et al., 2001), hybrid governance (Skelcher, 2005), and collaborative public management (Agranoff and McGuire, 2004). While there are nuances among these terms and the policy tools they emphasize, they share a consistent understanding about the role of government and public organizations in contemporary public administration and management. Across these terms, government is recognized as having political and legal authority to determine policies and their methods of implementation, and to appropriate resources for this implementation. Across these terms, bureaucracies are understood to labor in the pursuit of the public interest, which often requires engaging other governments, citizens, and private organizations (for-profit and nonprofit) in policy debates and in solutions for service delivery. Across these terms, it is recognized that as public organizations navigate complex policy problems, complex political dynamics, and complex resource deployment decisions, they will strategically form interdependencies with third party actors while steering the policy course and retaining oversight of those actors. While multi-sector collaboration is implicit in each of these terms, nonprofits figure most prominently in the concept of the hollow state. Milward and Provan's arguments were premised upon the notion that government's capacity to directly deliver services, mainly health and human services, had been largely supplanted by nonprofits. In this book, we examine the consequences of this reliance on nonprofits and to what extent it has delivered positive (or negative) outcomes, including public value for citizens. Therefore, "hollow state" is the conceptual frame from which we orient our analysis, and the term we engage throughout this book.

A number of different policy tools and financing instruments enable the state to function in this hollowed out condition. One of the most widely used mechanisms for delivering publicly funded services through nongovernmental organizations are fixed price and fee-for-service contracts. In the US, roughly 40 percent of the federal government's discretionary spending goes to contracts for goods and services, with the federal government spending more than $550 billion on these contracts in 2018, an increase of more than $100 billion from 2015 (US Government Accountability Office, 2019). While contracting is one of the more visible forms of outsourcing public functions, there are many other policy tools that facilitate a functioning hollowed out state, including grants, vouchers, and co-production. Grants are lump sum payments, often given to help subsidize administrative costs, to finance start-up costs of a new program, or pilot an innovative program model. Vouchers enable citizens to dictate the allocation of public funds, by choosing where to receive services among a set of providers in a community. Co-production is a process of engaging citizens, usually working as volunteers in the delivery of public services. Pestoff et al. (2012) describe co-production as a mix of activities in which bureaucratic professionals or "regular producers" act alongside citizens as voluntary "citizen producers" to enhance the quality and/or quantity of services they receive.

While the notion of hollowing out carries an undesirable connotation, many have theorized about the virtues of government reliance on nonprofits to perform public services. In many ways, the appeal of nonprofits as public service providers is intuitive. Nonprofits benefit from a "halo effect" in that they are viewed by citizens as among the most trustworthy institutions in society, and they enjoy bipartisan support. In a thorough and compelling fashion, Salamon (1995) articulated the benefits of the government–nonprofit service delivery partnership, describing it as a "win–win" for government as well as the nonprofit sector. Policymakers benefit by being able to meet constituents' needs through expanded services and increased government funding without increasing the size of the government workforce. Public bureaucracies benefit by capturing the flexibility, social innovation, and creative programming that may be highly effective in mitigating social or economic problems, but infeasible to implement in legally constrained, rule-bound bureaucracies. Bureaucracies contracting with nonprofits for services have the advantage of accessing professional expertise and capacity to address social problems that public organizations cannot address effectively on their own. As another form of added value, nonprofits can raise money through fundraising efforts, bringing their own resources to bear on social problems. Similarly, they provide spaces for citizens to volunteer and donate, generating "value added" labor and creating social capital in local communities. From their perspective, nonprofits benefit from the infusion of financial resources. Government funding enables nonprofits to expand the scope and scale of their operations and extend their missions to more people in need. It allows nonprofits to professionalize, build capacity, and to hire the most qualified employees. Government funding also confers upon nonprofits a degree of legitimacy, which positions them to compete more effectively for other types of institutional support such as foundation funding.

Despite these benefits there remains a persistent, underlying concern about the fragmentation of accountability under conditions of hollowed out service delivery, and questions remain about how best to assess the performance of these arrangements. In 2007, Frederickson and Frederickson published *Measuring the Performance of the Hollow State*, which offered an in-depth analysis of how five federal agencies within the US Department of Health and Human Services attempted to measure performance under severely hollowed out conditions. The public organizations in their study shared a common need to demonstrate responsiveness to the reforms of the federal Government Performance and Results Act (GPRA) of 1993, while faced with the reality that nearly all of their service delivery had been contracted out to third parties, namely nonprofit organizations. In their research, Frederickson and Frederickson (2007) found that these federal agencies collected a variety of performance data, both quantitative and qualitative, and relied on a wide variety of performance measures including process measures, outputs, fraud control measures, and annual reporting up the hierarchy and to political principals. Their study found that only one agency attempted to measure outcomes of service delivery. Thus, while we know that public organizations aim to capture various types of performance data even under hollowed out conditions, we ultimately know very little about the performance consequences, or outcomes that result from relying on nonprofits to deliver or co-produce public services.

Since the publication of Frederickson and Frederickson's study, demands for both public and nonprofit organizations to demonstrate accountability and performance have only intensified. As the hollow state became a recognized phenomenon and as residual NPM values linger in today's landscape of public service provision, nonprofits have faced increasing pressure to demonstrate their impact and outcomes. These pressures have come not only from the government agencies that fund nonprofits through taxpayer revenues, but also more recently from other institutional funders such as foundations, local inter-mediary funders such as United Ways, and from private citizens who donate precious time and money to these organizations.

Despite these pressures, and despite the growing adoption of performance measurement regimes within the nonprofit sector, there has been surprisingly little scholarly effort to examine the performance of nonprofit organizations as hollow state actors. Researchers have yet to demonstrate in any systematic way whether hollowing out the state and relying on nonprofits as service delivery partners yields positive benefits for service users, citizens, or the public more broadly. This is the central goal of our book. In the chapters that follow, we are concerned with the overarching questions: "How are nonprofits performing?" and "Does the presence or involvement of nonprofits in a public service improve public outcomes or otherwise add public value?" Through the chapters that follow, we aim to shed some light on these questions. We accomplish this through a diverse set of empirical studies spanning five local policy domains: public education, public health, urban sustainability, public parks and recreation, and public social welfare services. Our goal is to examine the performance of the nonprofit sector across these policy areas, and along the way to identify the factors that contribute to their success in mitigating public problems. We also identify challenges nonprofits encounter in their roles as government partners, and challenges that government organizations face in holding them to account for outcomes. In the next section, we review the literature on measuring performance in the nonprofit sector, followed by a discussion of what it means for nonprofits to generate public value. We then provide a brief overview of each chapter to guide readers through this book.

## CHALLENGES OF DEFINING AND MEASURING PERFORMANCE

Shaped in large part by the pressures encountered by nonprofit managers, no other topic has garnered more attention over the last decade in the nonprofit literature as the issue of performance. Researchers have approached the issue of nonprofit performance from a staggering variety of perspectives, examining questions that range from the technical and pragmatic, to the normative and philosophical. While the empirical studies are many and nuanced, we distill the nonprofit performance literature into three debates we regard as the most salient: (1) debates over the best methods and measures for evaluating perfor-mance; (2) debates over which actors should define performance, or who gets a say in how performance is to be assessed; (3) debates over how performance information should be used.

## Methods and Measures for Evaluating Performance: Is There a Best Way?

The most widely debated issue in the literature relates to methods and measures, and is fundamentally concerned with the question of how best to assess nonprofit performance. The question is both a technical and a normative one. To the extent they have measured performance at all, nonprofits have historically relied on output measures, counting for example the number of hot meals served, vaccines administered, or the number of free books or tutoring hours provided to low-income children in an after school program. Increasingly, however, nonprofits are pressured to measure outcomes, to demonstrate the impacts or effects of their programs and services (Mosley and Smith, 2018). One of the central challenges with designing performance systems to adequately capture outcomes is the difficulty of isolating the nonprofit program or service as the cause of improvement in the social condition that program is working to address. For example, the children participating in the after school tutoring program may indeed show improvements in academic performance, but a variety of factors might have led to this outcome, including increased support or help at home from caregivers, support from teachers, improved test-taking abilities, or their knowledge may simply have increased as a result of maturation. Or quite possibly, the children enrolled are inherently different in some way; having an advantage, for example, of their parents being sufficiently informed and motivated enough to enroll them in the program. In short, there are too many confounding influences to link with certainty improved school performance to the nonprofit after school program. This makes it difficult for the nonprofit to claim credit for its perceived program successes.

One way to address this outcome measurement problem is to restrict the program to a randomly chosen group of eligible children, and compare their outcomes against those who were not chosen to participate. Formal program evaluations and randomized control trials (RCTs) are methods of outcome measurement that use experimental designs, involving a set of clients or service recipients who have access to a program or service, where their outcomes or conditions are compared against those of an equivalently matched comparison group who have not had access to the program or service. These types of outcome measurement are superior in the sense that they can isolate the nonprofit program or service as the cause of improvement, but they are problematic for nonprofits in many ways. Nonprofits are mission-focused and typically want to extend their programming and services to as many people as possible; the notion of restricting their programming to a randomly chosen group for the sake of proving how well their program works is one that challenges the professional ethics of most nonprofit boards, managers, and frontline workers. Even if nonprofit leaders could be persuaded to adopt this type of measurement, the cost of carrying it out represents a formidable barrier. MacIndoe and Barman (2012) found that more than half of nonprofits implementing performance measures of some sort do so without any resources budgeted for them. Moreover, the vast majority of nonprofits lack the expertise and technical capacity in-house to carry out an RCT, and thus have to outsource this program evaluation, often to a university researcher or some other type of evaluation expert, at a substantial cost to the organization. Experimental approaches can more readily isolate cause and effect relationships between nonprofit services and outcomes, but the use of these methods has been slow to diffuse.

Another promising method of assessing impact for nonprofits involves social return on investment (SROI) measures, which rely on a modified form of cost–benefit analysis. The benefits of this approach include monetizing social value generated by nonprofit programs, forcing nonprofits to take a critical look at their own costs, conveying to legislators (who appropriate public funds for the services) the long-term cost savings to the public as a result of investment, and signalling to donors a clear return for each dollar invested. However, this form of performance measurement has been fraught with challenges and slow to catch on in the US, and adopted with only slightly greater frequency in Europe. In addition to resource limitations and capacity constraints, Moody et al. (2015) cite some of the challenges associated with implementing SROI measures, including "selecting the right group of stakeholders to define impact measures, building consensus around indicators and measurement techniques, determining the portion of an observed change that is due to the activities under consideration, overcoming resource limitations and the lack of incentives, and dealing with inadequate commitment among stakeholders" (p. 29).

While there is wide variation in the types of performance measures that nonprofits use, there is a growing consensus that capturing outcomes is preferable to capturing outputs. In light of this, there have been a few industry-level initiatives to standardize metrics for assessing nonprofit program performance, such as the Urban Institutes' Outcomes Indicator Project. Through this initiative, a team of evaluation experts developed a set of outcomes across 14 programs common among nonprofits, such as assisted living, health risk reduction, prisoner re-entry, job training, community organizing, and youth mentoring. The goal of this initiative was not only to offer nonprofits working in these program areas a ready-to-use resource to encourage internal performance measurement programs, but also to provide funders a way to compare outcomes among organizations providing similar services (Lampkin et al.,

2007). While this initiative showed promise for helping nonprofits overcome some of the expertise and capacity challenges that have limited nonprofits from implementing performance measurement programs, the initiative never expanded and many nonprofit leaders remain unaware of its existence. Other efforts have included toolkits by state nonprofit associations to help their member organizations develop outcome measures so as to more effectively message to the public about their impact, and enhance prospects for funding. However, these initiatives have been limited to only a handful of states such as Illinois, Minnesota, and New York. In short, the vast majority of nonprofits do not measure outcomes, restrict their measures only to outputs, and lack aware-ness of existing tools and resources to help build performance measurement capacity. At the same time, they remain very much aware of the pressure to capture outcome data to demonstrate their value to the public.

While there is consensus about the importance of capturing quantifiable outcomes, there is also agreement among scholars that perceptual aspects of performance, such as client satisfaction, are also important and should not be discounted. Scholars agree that nonprofit performance is multidimensional and no single outcome indicator can adequately capture the complexity of nonprofit performance (Thomson, 2010; MacIndoe and Barman, 2012; Sowa et al., 2004). Given the wide range of stakeholder perspectives and complexity of most nonprofit missions, many scholars have called for a multidimen-sional approach to measuring nonprofit performance. Sowa et al. (2004), for example, state that "hidden behind outcome measurements are complex and diverse dynamics that may vary across and within organizations and programs," arguing that "both objective and perceptual measures are needed to fully capture the dimensions of effectiveness." These authors advocate for a multidimensional and integrated model of nonprofit organizational effectiveness that should take into account managerial capacity, program outcomes, organizational financial health, and employee satisfaction. On the program dimension, the authors suggest client satisfaction, along with objec-tive indicators of outcome measures related to a specific program consistent with the program's theory of change, and managerial perceptions of program performance. Thomson (2010) conceptualizes multidimensionality in terms of the number, collection frequency, and complexity of outcome measures, while MacIndoe and Barman (2012) define it as a combined assessment from resource providers (for example, funding agencies such as government organizations and foundations), organizational networks (accrediting bodies, nonprofit associations, federations,) and internal stakeholders (for example, boards) who collectively influence the use and resources available for outcome measurement.

Hence, while outcome measures are important, they do not constitute a sin-gular or "best way" of assessing nonprofit performance. The multidimensionality of nonprofit performance is driven in large part by the reality that these organizations must account to multiple stakeholders, and various stakeholder groups may define and value performance differently. And this brings us to the next major debate in the nonprofit performance literature, which is the question of who, or which groups, has a legitimate claim to defining and assessing nonprofit performance.

## Who Defines and Shapes Nonprofit Performance?

Another major theme in the nonprofit performance literature relates to the question of who should be involved in the process of defining performance; which can include playing a role in the design of performance measures, capturing performance data, or processing its meaning through analysis or evaluation. Nonprofit stakeholders rely on different indicators to judge performance, but these indicators might produce conflicting evidence of "good" performance. For example, from the perspective of nonprofit board members, financial cuts that result in cost savings and a balanced budget for the organization may be viewed as an indicator of positive organizational performance, but if those cost savings come at the expense of staff benefits or reduced investment in staff training, it may undermine personnel performance and cause the organization to be perceived as a poorly performing employer by employee stakeholders. Similarly, funders of nonprofit organizations often impose measures of performance that conflict with the organization's own definitions of performance. For example, a local public health authority that contracts with a nonprofit for community based mental health care may evaluate contractor performance by the number of days the nonprofit utilized inpatient psychiatric hospitals stays for its clients, a costly form of treatment making other alternatives preferable. This creates an incentive for the nonprofit's leaders and frontline staff to restrict this form of treatment, even in scenarios where they believe it is clinically in the best interest of clients and their families.

Campbell and Lambright (2016) propose a multiple constituency theory of performance, arguing that reporting obligations of funders tend to disproportionately shape the ways nonprofit leaders define and measure performance. This focus on complying with funder-imposed performance requirements often means that nonprofit leaders overlook or minimize other important sources of performance feedback, such as input from their own frontline staff, or from service recipients. The multiple constituency approach is consistent with the spirit of the multidimensional approach; the former emphasizes input from multiple people or stakeholder groups, while the latter emphasizes reliance on multiple outcome measures, which can include input derived from different stakeholder groups. The multiple constituency theory and combined literature on multidimensionality prescribe four sets of actors that play critical roles in defining, shaping and assessing nonprofit performance: funders, non-profit leaders (including board members), frontline staff, and nonprofit clients/patrons.

As the hollow state metaphor suggests, funders play perhaps the most important role in dictating nonprofit performance, often by prescribing in contract language what gets measured and how often. Campbell and Lambright (2016) argue that "because of resource dependencies, reporting obligations developed by funders play a large role in defining performance and determining the measures providers use." And there is ample evidence to support this contention. In a national study of nonprofit human service providers, LeRoux and Wright (2010) found that greater reliance on institutional funding sources (government, foundations, intermediaries) increased the adoption and use of performance measures by nonprofits. In another survey of nonprofits' evaluation activities, Carman and Fredericks (2008) found that 71 percent of nonprofits that engaged in some form of performance measurement produced reports for funders about financial expenditures related to program activities. Thomson (2010) studied the impact of government mandates on nonprofit propensity to measure and convey performance, and found that the threat of losing government funding was highly effective in motivating nonprofits to institute performance measurement programs. His study relayed how the city of Detroit, under pressure from the federal Housing and Urban Development agency (HUD), threatened to eliminate funding to nonprofits which failed to adopt performance measures and demonstrate outcomes. Thomson reports that the city's nonprofit sector prior to the mandate was less successful in measuring actual outcomes than it was in identifying hoped-for outcomes. Unsurprisingly, he found that after the mandate, many more organizations began implementing performance measures, and by five years after the mandate, roughly half of all the nonprofits were able to identify at least one specific, observable outcome.

While mandates and requirements of funders might account for the single biggest factor in nonprofits' performance measurement efforts, it may have the unintended consequence of diverting scarce administrative resources to capturing data that organizational leaders do not find useful. In an ideal scenario, nonprofit funders such as government organizations and foundation program officers would consult with the leaders of their nonprofit contract, and grant recipients to negotiate what gets measured, to ensure the types of data that are captured are mutually beneficial. Nonprofit leaders and board members also play a key role in defining and measuring performance. Using data from a national survey of nonprofit human service organizations, LeRoux and Langer (2016) find that boards play a role in establishing and measuring organizational performance, although executive directors generally would prefer even higher levels of board engagement in these activities. In another study of government–nonprofit partnerships, Gazley (2010) found that "the strongest association to real performance improvement comes from the intensity of shared goals and the level of investment in the partnership." She finds the strongest predictors of effectiveness to include the level of goal agreement between government and nonprofit actors, and age of the partnership, pointing to the importance of time for relationships to form. Yet all too often performance goals are dictated to nonprofit leaders by funding agencies without any negotiation or discussion (LeRoux and Wright, 2010).

Although considered with far less frequency in the nonprofit performance literature, frontline staff represent another critical constituency involved in performance measurement. Benjamin and Campbell (2014) have demonstrated that frontline workers in human service nonprofits play instrumental roles in nonprofit performance by supporting clients in achieving desired outcomes through a process they call "co-determination." Similar in concept to co-production, co-determination relies on frontline workers to develop partnerships with clients, define desired outcomes and strategies collectively with clients, and support client capacity to take positive action for change. Highlighting the role that nonprofit clients and service users play in shaping performance outcomes, Benjamin and Campbell emphasize the role of client agency in the process: performance gains through co-determination cannot be achieved by frontline workers alone. They argue that "clients are active agents whose desires, attitudes, needs and situational constraints play key roles in the change process" (2014, p. 989). Their arguments and findings align with others, such as Corrigan (2006), who offers evidence from mental health and elder care studies revealing that consumer-led service models lead to improved recovery outcomes for clients.

While frontline workers can thus play important roles in shaping nonprofit performance, their understanding of organizational performance goals should not be assumed. In their national study of child welfare organizations, Jolles et al. (2017) found that fewer than half of managers reported that their frontline workers had a strong understanding of the agency's performance measures. These authors conclude that managerial communication and board involvement in performance measurement are key predictors of frontline worker understanding of performance measures. Thus the burden falls on nonprofit leaders to create a performance culture, even when the measures are dictated from the outside. Nonprofit leaders can strive for such a culture through transparency, positive messaging about performance measurement, securing staff buy-in, and providing sufficient training and feedback to frontline workers so they fully understand their role in organizational and program performance measurement.

Finally, nonprofit clients, service users, and patrons also shape performance measurement practices. In addition to their roles in co-determination work, nonprofit clients and service users can also play a role in shaping nonprofit performance efforts by serving on nonprofit governing boards, task forces, and advisory councils (LeRoux, 2009a). Moreover, the majority of nonprofits collect some form of client or customer satisfaction data. Morley et al. (2001) examined the use of client surveys by nonprofits and found that approximately 78 percent of nonprofits conducted client surveys designed to measure satisfaction, client outcomes to be used as performance measures, or both. These authors further found that about half of these surveys also collected information from clients on other aspects of service quality, such as timeliness of service provision and helpfulness of staff (Morley et al., 2001). Similarly, Carman and Fredericks (2008) found that 67 percent of nonprofits collect data on consumer or participant satisfaction on a regular basis. However, there is evidence to suggest that client feedback is generally not accorded the same value or given the same weight as that of other stakeholders. LeRoux and Wright (2010) found that among six different types of performance data collected by nonprofits, client satisfaction data was the only type not statistically linked to decision-making by nonprofit leaders. Similarly, LeRoux (2009b) found that when nonprofit clients are paying customers, nonprofits become more responsive to their input, but when nonprofits receive indirect payments for those clients, nonprofit leaders allocate more of their time and attention to ensuring responsiveness to those entities that do pay. These facts underscore that while nonprofit service users do play a role in defining performance, their input remains somewhat marginalized and is not a reliable predictor of how well the nonprofit might be performing on other measures. This also brings us to our final debate in the nonprofit performance literature, which is how performance data and information should be used.

## How Should Nonprofit Performance Information Be Used?

The third critical debate in the nonprofit performance literature relates to the question of who benefits from capturing nonprofit performance data, along with whether and how this performance information should be used. In theory, managers develop and implement performance measurement systems to document how well they are doing, identify areas for improvement, and improve decision-making (Moynihan, 2005). From the vantage point of institutional funders such as government, performance information might help identify areas where capacity building and technical support are needed among seemingly lower-performing nonprofit contract partners. From the perspective of nonprofit leaders, it is presumed that performance information will be used to identify inefficiencies, optimize personnel resources, and make necessary adjustments to services and program implementation. Yet given that performance measures are often imposed by outside funders, it remains unclear to what extent nonprofit organizational leaders can use the performance data they have collected in any meaningful way. On one hand, LeRoux and Wright (2010) found that the range of performance measures used by nonprofits was positively linked to improved strategic decision-making by nonprofit leaders. On the other hand, Carman and Fredericks (2008) found fully one-third of all nonprofit employees view evaluation of their programs and services as a "resource drain and distraction," making it unlikely that managers will make use of data, even if forced to collect it. These authors also found that some nonprofit managers view performance measurement as a strategic planning tool, and others view it simply as a marketing and promotional tool (Carman and Fredericks, 2008).

Another central question that relates to the use of performance information is whether it should be used by funders in resource distribution or allocation decisions. Will performance data be used by funders to reward nonprofits that appear to meet all their pre-established performance goals, and punish those which do not? Will data be used by funding principals to compare performance across contractors in a provider network, and if so, to what end? Linking incentives to and penalties to performance is fraught with challenges, and yet performance-based contracting is a fairly common practice by government organizations. All too often these arrangements lead to problems of "cream skimming" or incentivizing nonprofits to admit/treat/take the easiest clients, leaving a gap in the market for the most difficult and problematic. When imperfect performance measures are tied to financial incentives, it can easily lead to "performance perversity" (Moynihan, 2014), a situation that incentivizes actors to "game the system." For example, a private nonprofit charter school might tout its high graduation rate as a measure of performance in order to attract more voucher "customers," but indiscriminately pass students in order to appear high-performing. Dias and Maynard-Moody (2006) described a similar challenge of performance-based pay arrangements in a study examining outcomes for job training recipients in a welfare-to-work program. With organizational financial incentives tied to the performance outcome of job placement for program recipients, workers were encouraged by managers to steer people into easy-to-find low-paying jobs, rather than pursue extended training or education that might have led to a higher-paying job and greater economic self-sufficiency in the long term. Dias and Maynard-Moody describe this as a "performance paradox": the same efforts made to meet contractually imposed performance metrics ironically produce negative program practice and poorer client outcomes, "doing little to reduce long-term welfare use or diminish recipients' poverty." Hence, while use of performance information to distribute financial incentives to nonprofits by their funders may appear as a logical way to incentivize performance in theory, the unintended consequences of these arrangements may outweigh any potential performance improvements.

## NONPROFITS AND PUBLIC VALUE CREATION

Given the complexities and challenges associated with measuring nonprofit performance, another way to think about performance in the hollow state is through the lens of public value. Indeed, Bryson et al. (2014) suggest that public value can serve as a performance measurement and management framework, pointing out via Kalambokidis (2014) that an advantage of the public value idea is that there is no single bottom line. Thus, as a perspective for evaluating the performance of hollow state arrangements, it is consistent with the nonprofit performance literature reviewed earlier, which concluded there is no single best measure or metric, and it is informed by a variety of stakeholder perspectives. A robust body of scholarly work has emerged from public interest theory on organizational publicness (Bozeman and Moulton, 2011), and public value (Moore, 1995; Stoker, 2006; Bozeman, 2007). So extensive is this literature that it would be impossible to review it in the space of this chapter. For readers wishing to delve further into this broad expanse of work, we would direct them to Van der Wal et al.'s (2013) meta-analysis of public values research, based on 397 articles. Here, we will simply define what is meant by public value and consider some of the insights from the literature most relevant to public values in the context of the hollow state.

In tracing the history of public interest theory, Bozeman (2007) argues that public interest represents more of an ideal, while public values have "specific, identifiable content" (p. 12). He defines the public interest as "the outcomes best serving the long-run survival and well-being of a social collective construed as a 'public'" (2007, p. 12), while he defines public values as "normative consensus about a) the rights, benefits, and prerogatives to which citizens and should (and should not) be entitled; b) the obligations of citizens to society, the state, and to one another; and c) the principles upon which governments and policies should be based" (2007, p. 13). Whereas Bozeman focuses on the society or policy level, Mark Moore (1995) focuses more on the role of the public manager in creating public value (Bryson et al., 2014). Moore's (1995, 2014) basic premise is that if the primary objective of private firms is to produce shareholder value, then the central goal of public managers should commensurately be to create public value. His conception of public value encompasses both traditional values of efficiency and effectiveness of public bureaucracies, but also emphasizes procedural and substantive justice. Thus, assessing whether public value has been created from Moore's perspective requires some combination of input, process, output, and outcome measures.

Moore (1995) conceives of public value as value creation, and role of managers is central to that process. He asserts that:

> Public managers create public value. The problem is that they cannot know for sure what that is … It is not enough to say that public managers create results that are valued; they must be able to show that the results obtained are worth the cost of private consumption and unrestrained liberty forgone in producing the desirable results. Only then can we be sure that some public value has been created. (Moore, 1995, pp. 57, 29)

Moore offers a strategic triangle to be employed by managers in their calculus of public value creation. He argues that strategy: (1) must be aimed at achieving something substantively valuable (must have or create public value); (2) must be legitimate (that is, politically feasible); and (3) must be operationally and administratively feasible (Moore, 1995, pp. 22–23). Additionally, Moore (2014) proposes the concept of "public value accounting" for public managers to ascertain whether and how public value has been created. In the process of public value accounting, he suggests that managers need to look at costs and benefits as well as at less tangible aspects of value when they assess public value creation (Moore, 2014). Thus, while early foundational works on the topic of public values and public value accounting offered broad conceptualizations of these ideas, they lack specific direction for measuring public value creation, and as Bryson et al. (2014) point out, these early voices are largely silent on the role of nonprofits in public value creation. Scholars have expanded upon this work more recently (Moulton and Eckerd, 2012; Stoker, 2006; Aldridge and Stoker, 2002) to offer more specific indicators by which we might assess public value creation. We shall examine these in greater detail shortly.

**Public Values in the Hollow State**

Drawing on Bozeman and Moore's work, Bryson et al. (2014), propose a new paradigm that they term "public value governance" for today's era of managing contract and multi-sector networked arrangements. These authors contrast public value governance with traditional public administration and its successor, new public management (NPM), arguing that different values are accorded greater priority in each of these paradigms. They argue efficiency to be the key value characterizing traditional public administration; efficiency and effectiveness to be the main values underlying new public management; while "efficiency, effectiveness, and the full range of democratic and constitutional values" characterize this new era of public value governance (2014, p. 446). Accordingly, they see the need for public managers to demonstrate adherence to an increased range of accountability mechanisms, including not only the "old" NPM type mandates for performance reporting, but also to an expanded range of interests including citizens, community values, political norms, and professional standards. Under this new paradigm of public value governance, public values are less determined by political goals and legislative priorities, but rather determined through a process of negotiation led by public agencies, involving deliberation and dialogue with citizens, community groups, private organizations, and other stakeholders. Thus the new public governance is both process and outcome oriented.

The notion of public value governance was derived in part from earlier work by Stoker (2006), who argued that "public value management" is the new paradigm for the contemporary hollow and networked state, replacing new public management and traditional public management. Stoker (2006) defines the public interest in the public value management paradigm as "individual and public preferences produced through a complex process of interaction that involves deliberative reflection over inputs and opportunity costs." Stoker argues that public value management must answer three core questions about what it will deliver when it comes to efficiency, accountability, and equity, and how it will deliver benefits in these areas. His emphasis on negotiated goal setting and developing citizen capacity for the expression of individual rights and responsibilities is very consistent with those articulated by Bryson et al. (2014). Stoker's position on the important role of managers in creating public value parallels those of Moore (1995), but Stoker situates his arguments more squarely in the context of the hollow state.

Stoker argued for the field to place a greater premium on a public service ethos rather than a public sector ethic. He envisions this public sector ethos as transcending sector distinctions, serving as a moral guide not only for public managers tasked with procurement of services, but also for those working in private for-profit or nonprofit organizations tasked with public service. He argues:

> there is no ideological dimension to deciding who provides services and no particular moral virtue in people receiving their wages directly from the government. The assumption is that although direct provision from within the organization may be appropriate in some circumstances, in many others the advantages of private or voluntary sector provision will be greater. The private sector, for example, may be able to combine vitally needed investment with the responsibility for providing services. The voluntary sector, through its wider involvements, may be able to guarantee a more joined-up or seamless service for the public. Above all, what public value management expects is for a relational approach to service procurement. There should not be a great divide between client and contractor; both should see each other as partners looking to sustain relationship over the long run and should not be narrowly focused on any contract. (Stoker, 2006, p. 48)

In assessing public value creation, Stoker (2006) calls for pluralist stakeholder review of hollow state actors, and also calls for benchmarking and open competition in the procurement process.

Using slightly different terminology, Bozeman too pointed to "manifestations of market-based policies" such as privatization, contracting, use of vouchers, and government management of contractors as fundamentally changing the meaning of "publicness" (Bozeman, 2007). Building on this idea, Bozeman and Moulton (2011) argue that "just as organizations and policies can be evaluated by the extent to which they are constrained or enabled by political and economic authority, policies and organizations can also be evaluated by the extent to which they achieve public values"; a process described by Moulton (2009) as "realized publicness." While the concepts of realized publicness, public value, achievement, and public value accounting remain somewhat diffuse, based on our rendering of the literature, we attempt in the next section to narrow in on some specific attributes we might look for in determining whether public value has been created by the hollow state.

**Specific, Identifiable Content of Public Values**

Bozeman argued that public values have "specific, identifiable content" (Bozeman, 2007, p. 12), and while he makes no mention of how we might extract this content from hollow state arrangements, we make some inferences from the literature throughout this book to guide our assessment of performance and public value in the hollow state. First, we would point to Aldridge and Stoker's (2002) five elements comprising a common set of public values shared by those engaged in public sector service delivery: a performance culture, a commitment to accountability, a capacity to support universal access, responsible employment practices, and contribution to community well-being. When we see these attributes present, we consider this to be public value creation, and we balance this against traditional perspectives of performance. Relatedly, Moulton and Eckerd (2012) theorized that specific resource streams may shape nonprofits' value systems, positing that greater reliance on government funding institutionalizes public value within nonprofits. They developed and tested a "nonprofit sector role index" consisting of six expressions of public value: service delivery, innovation, advocacy, individual expression, social capital creation, and citizen engagement. When we see these attributes present, we also consider this to be public value creation, and similarly consider these benefits alongside traditional perspectives of nonprofit performance. Finally, we consider some indicators of public value creation suggested by Bryson et al. (2014). When we observe in hollow state arrangements instances of citizens acting as problem-solvers or co-creators actively engaged in what is valued by the public, instances of civic learning and/or building civic capacity, and instances of citizens shaping policy through dialogue and deliberation, we consider this, too, to be public value creation. In our assessment of performance in the hollow state, we thus consider traditional perspectives on how performance is measured, but also whether some degree of public value is generated by these arrangements, using the "identifiable content" specified here.

## OUTLINE FOR THIS BOOK

Toward the conclusion of their seminal work elaborating the concept of the hollow state, Milward and Provan pose the question: "Is the hollow state better or worse than the bureaucratic state? This is a question that at present cannot be answered" (Milward and Provan, 2000, p. 364). While we may never be able to definitively answer this question, we have more answers today than we did 20 years ago. The public management of today calls for a different question. The question is no longer one of whether "private provider or government is better" but whether, and to what extent, public value exists today under the conditions of hollow state. And looking to the future, how can public organizations best foster public value creation in the design of outsourced service delivery arrangements? In this book, we attempt to shed light on these questions.

To this end, we have assembled a set of empirical studies that allow us to take stock of performance and public value in the hollow state. While the majority of these studies are set in the context of the US, and one in Europe, the themes of this book are applicable to most countries in which the state relies heavily on the nonprofit sector and/or voluntary organizations to deliver public services. Each of the following chapters in this book examines a different local policy or public service area. These works were intentionally selected to showcase the breadth of nonprofit involvement in local public service delivery. While many people tend to associate the government–nonprofit partnership with social welfare provision, governments enlist the aid of nonprofits to carry out a variety of local services and policy objectives. We selected studies for this book that represent some of these lesser-known, yet highly common partnerships with nonprofits for services spanning K-12 (kindergarten to 12th grade) public education, parks and recreation services, public health, and community development, as well as social welfare. These chapters were also selected for their methodological diversity, creatively employing new and interesting data, both qualitative and quantitative. Each empirical chapter not only examines nonprofit performance in a different policy or service area, but also highlights a different policy tool or financing mechanism that governments use to carry out services through nonprofits, including vouchers, fee-for-service contracts, and government-supporting charitable foundations, a form of co-production.

Collectively, these studies help us to answer the question of whether and how nonprofits improve public service outcomes or otherwise create public value.

Here we offer a brief overview of each chapter, in an effort to provide readers with a road map for the rest of the book and to highlight the service and/or policy areas that are the focus of study in each. Every chapter represents a self-contained study; it is not necessary to read them in sequence. While we hope that readers find value in the entire book, this overview is designed to provide an information shortcut of sorts to those who may wish to skip around or begin at the chapter or policy issue of greatest interest to them.

Chapter 2 presents the first of these empirical studies. In this chapter, Michael Ford examines the ability of nonprofit charter schools to effectively address the "wicked problem" of urban public education. This case is set in the city of Milwaukee, home to the oldest and largest school choice voucher program in the US, and where about 40 percent of publicly funded K-12 students attend a nonprofit voucher or charter school. The use of vouchers as a mechanism for distributing government funding is rooted in public choice logic. In theory, allowing consumer choice to shape the market for local public education should force education providers to compete in ways that improve service quality. Yet, the results of Ford's study demonstrate the flaws in this logic, and highlight the difficulty of holding government-funded service providers to account when public funding is not conditioned upon clear performance expectations, but relies instead upon market forces. Absent any imposed performance or accountability measures, and given the highly market-driven nature of this public good, Ford uses school closures as the measure of accountability. The logic suggests that when schools exhibit poor performance, parents will send their children to another, better-performing school and eventually the low-performing schools will be selected out of the market. Using a panel dataset of publicly funded nonprofit schools spanning four years, Ford's survival analysis reveals that while enrollment growth and other organizational factors can reduce closure rates, student outcomes on reading and math proficiency have no relationship to charter school failure. In other words, nonprofit schools failing in their educational mission face no real consequences for their low performance.

Chapter 3 presents the case of public health, examining whether hollow state health care actors perform in ways that improve health outcomes at the community level. In this chapter, Zhao and LeRoux offer results from a national study of service contracting by over a thousand local public health departments (LHDs) across the US. The consequences of contracting have been studied extensively, but as the authors point out, most of the research to date has been concerned with the efficiency question: that is, whether or to what extent contracting reduces costs. Zhao and LeRoux speak to a lesser-studied contracting question which is that of effectiveness: whether contracting yields better service quality or improved outcomes. Working from theoretical perspectives of transaction costs, the authors theorize that outsourcing may improve service quality, but only under ideal conditions in which the services being contracted are characterized by low transaction costs. The authors examine contracting for four types of health services which vary in their degree of transaction costs: mental health prevention; treatment for HIV/AIDS and other sexually transmitted infections; pregnancy prevention; and regulation of tobacco retailers and enforcement of smoking ordinances. To examine the impact of contracting for each of these functions, the authors combine survey data capturing contracting decisions from the National Profile of Local Health Department Study collected by the National Association of County and City Health Officials, and pair it with outcome data from County Health Rankings and Roadmaps (CHRR), for four corresponding health outcomes at the county level: frequent mental distress, sexually transmitted infections, teen births, and adult smoking rates. The findings indicate that contracting out lower transaction cost services is more likely to reduce risks of contract failure and produce better health outcomes.

In Chapter 4, Nathaniel Wright and Tony Reames examine the role of community action agencies (CAAs) in contributing to the sustainability of distressed neighborhoods. Originating through the federal War on Poverty funds during the 1960s, CAAs were an important fixture in American communities long before the concept of a hollow state emerged. For nearly seven decades, CAAs have provided for basic needs such as housing, and stimulating economic investment and opportunity in impoverished communities that markets have largely failed to serve. However, the mission of these organizations has evolved over time to include a much wider array of services and public responsibilities. Community sustainability represents one area where CAAs have played an increasingly important role in recent years. CAAs have assumed responsibility for many aspects of sustainable development, including residential weatherization, energy conservation, transportation, and the provision of housing and shelter to urban and rural communities. In light of this, Wright and Reames set out to identify the factors that shape the effectiveness of CAAs in creating sustainable communities, through a study of these organizations situated in major US cities. They find that community engagement, human resource capacity, county/regional government collaboration, government funding, and revenue diversification are important predictors of CAAs' community sustainability performance. These findings have important implications: government funding drives nonprofits to perform better, yet government does not have to bear the entire funding burden in order to have this effect. Their results further suggest that citizen participation, a fundamental public value, contributes to greater effectiveness when it is embraced and implemented by nonprofit leaders.

Authors Daniel Cheng, Yu Shi, and Simon Andrew take a somewhat different approach to the government–nonprofit partnership in Chapter 5, by examining how private philanthropic foundations help to raise funds for public parks and whether this philanthropic support enhances performance of the park system. The growth of private nonprofit foundations that raise funds for government organizations underfunded by tax revenues is a trend that has been studied in several contexts including national parks (Yandle et al., 2016), K-12 public schools (Nelson and Gazely, 2014), and public libraries (Schatteman and Bingle, 2015). Cheng and his colleagues examine park-supporting foundations, also known as "friends of the park" groups, as a form of co-production. Their study documents the growth of charitable support for public parks in the face of declining public revenues, and examines the link between this private funding and performance of public park systems. They measure performance by capturing park acreage, public access, and outputs (play structures and facilities). Studying the 68 largest city park systems in the US, they find that total spending by nonprofit groups largely has a positive effect on city park performance. Another important factor driving city park performance is education level of the population, suggesting that citizen demand-making is also important. However, these authors point to several equity implications of their findings. These authors also caution us that while philanthropic support might supplement public appropriations and user fees at the margins, it is not a substitute for tax revenue. If citizens want more and better parks, they will have to make demands of city government, and if nonprofit parks groups can help spur this mobilization, they are helping to create public value through increased citizen engagement.

In Chapter 6, Peter Raeymaeckers and Peter Cools examine an increasingly common dilemma confronted by government-funded social service providers, which is the pressure to demonstrate their performance through measurable outcomes as a condition of continued funding. Many nonprofits confronted with the scenario simply acquiesce to externally imposed performance metrics demanded by their government funders, even if leaders believe these measures to be inadequate for capturing the organization's impact or, worse, a waste of managerial effort. The reality is that many nonprofits feel powerless to question their government funders, since their current and future funding may be threatened by challenging these measures. Yet, Raeymaeckers and Cools demonstrate how an organized, strategic effort among a collective of social service organizations tasked with combatting poverty successfully challenged a new mandate for funder-imposed performance measures, and instead negotiated a process with their subsidizing government to determine how performance should be measured. Their study is situated in the Belgian city of Antwerp and examines a network of social service organizations known as "associations where people in poverty lift up their voice." Using qualitative data from interviews and focus groups with agency coordinators, social workers, people in poverty who receive services, and representatives from the local government who fund the providers, Raeymaekers and Cool yield illustrative findings that depart from the conventional approach of acquiescence, and might serve as a guide for other nonprofits that strive for negotiated performance assessment with their funders. They reveal a range of tactics used by social service providers in this process, including using the power of their own professional expertise not only as a form of control, but also as a form of resistance and for promoting the values of a social service organization, especially the value of participatory practices and client inclusion. In doing so, they conclude that social service providers might achieve a more balanced approach to performance measurement that takes into account process, as well as more diverse range of stakeholder perspectives including those of clients.

Finally, in Chapter 7, we distill the lessons offered by these studies for governing the future of the hollow state and propose a new framework for integrating traditional performance measures with measurement of public value creation. We frame our discussion with the ultimate objective of aiding policymakers and public sector leaders in the design of their partnerships with non-governmental organizations in ways that yield the best deal for the public. We highlight consistencies in these studies that point to themes for enhancing the accountability, performance, effectiveness, and public value creation of third-party organizations involved in the production and delivery of public services. We also highlight consistencies in the evidence with regard to challenges faced by these organizations in achieving their goals, including capacity issues, funding issues, and government disinvestment, along with flaws in the design of current accountability and oversight mechanisms. We also discuss roles for the public and individual citizens, including specific ways they can engage with these organizations to help improve nonprofits' accountability, performance, and public value.

## NOTE

1.  While the term "hollow state" diffused widely with the publication of Milward and Provan's 2000 article, it was introduced earlier by the authors in their book chapter titled "The hollow state: Private provision of public services" (Milward and Provan, 1993). Others had introduced the concept even earlier, although using different terminology, such as the "shadow state" (Wolch, 1990).

## REFERENCES

Agranoff, R., and McGuire, M. (2004). *Collaborative Public Management: New Strategies for Local Governments*. Washington, DC: Georgetown University Press.

Aldridge, R., and Stoker, G. (2002). *Advancing a New Public Service Ethos*. London: New Local Government Network (NLGN).

Benjamin, L., and Campbell, D. (2014). Nonprofit performance: Accounting for the agency of clients. *Nonprofit and Voluntary Sector Quarterly*, 44: 988–1006.

Bozeman, B. (2007). *Public Values and Public Interest: Counterbalancing Economicindividualism*. Washington, DC: Georgetown University Press.

Bozeman, B., and Moulton, S. (2011). Integrative publicness: A framework for public management strategy and performance. *Journal of Public Administration Research and Theory*, 21(1): 363–380.

Bryson, J.M., Crosby, B.S., and Bloomberg, L. (2014). Public value governance: Moving beyond traditional Public Administration and the New Public Management. *Public Administration Review*, 74(4): 445–456.

Campbell, D.A., and Lambright, K. (2016). Program performance and multiple constituency theory. *Nonprofit and Voluntary Sector Quarterly*, 45(1): 150–171.

Carman, J.G., and Fredericks, K.A. (2008). Nonprofits and evaluation: Empirical evidence from the field. *Nonprofits and Evaluation: New Directions for Evaluation*, 119: 51–71.

Corrigan, P. (2006). Impact of consumer-operated services on empowerment and recovery of people with psychiatric disabilities. *Psychiatric Services*, 57: 1493–1496.

Dias, J.J., and Maynard-Moody, S. (2006). For-profit welfare: Contracts, conflicts, and the performance paradox. *Journal of Public Administration Research and Theory*, 17: 189–211

Frederickson, D.G., and Frederickson, H.G. (2007). *Measuring the Performance of the Hollow State*. Washington, DC: Georgetown University Press.

Frederickson, H.G. (1999). The repositioning of American Public Administration. *PS: Political Science and Politics*, 32: 701–711.

Gazley, B. (2010). Linking collaborative capacity to performance measurement in government–nonprofit partnerships. *Nonprofit and Voluntary Sector Quarterly*, 39(4): 653–673.

Jolles, M.P., Collins-Carmago, C., McBeath, B., Bunger, A.C., and Chuang, E. (2017). Managerial strategies to influence frontline worker understanding of performance measures in nonprofit child welfare agencies. *Nonprofit and Voluntary Sector Quarterly*, 46(6): 1166–1188.

Kalambokidis, L. (2014). Creating public value with tax and spending policies: The view from public economics. *Public Administration Review*, 74(4): 519–26.

Lampkin, L.L., Winkler, M.K., Kirlin, J., Hatry, H.P., Natenshon, D., et al. (2007). *Building a Common Outcome Framework to Measure Nonprofit Performance*. Washington, DC: Urban Institute.

LeRoux, K. (2009a). Paternalistic or participatory governance? Examining opportunities for client participation in nonprofit social service organizations, *Public Administration Review*, 69(3): 504–517.

LeRoux, K. (2009b). Managing stakeholder demands: Balancing responsiveness to clients and funding agents in nonprofit social service organizations. *Administration and Society*, 41(2): 158–184.

LeRoux, K., and Wright, N. (2010). Does performance measurement improve strategic decision making? Findings from a national survey of nonprofit social service agencies. *Nonprofit and Voluntary Sector Quarterly*, 39: 571–587.

LeRoux, K., and Langer, J. (2016). Explaining the gap between what nonprofit executives want and what they get from board members. *Nonprofit Management and Leadership*, 27(2): 147–164.

Lynn, L.E., Heinrich, C., and Hill, C. (2001). *Improving Governance: A New Logic for Empirical Research.* Washington, DC: Georgetown University Press.

MacIndoe, H., and Barman, E. (2012). How organizational stakeholders shape performance measurement in nonprofits: Exploring a multidimensional measure. *Nonprofit and Voluntary Sector Quarterly*, 42(4): 716–738.

Milward, H.B., and Provan, K.G. (1993). The hollow state: Private provision of public services. In H. Ingram and S.R. Smith (eds), *Public Policy for Democracy.* Washington, DC: Brookings Institution, pp. 222–237.

Milward, H.B., and Provan, K.G. (2000). Governing the hollow state. *Journal of Public Administration Research and Theory*, 10(2): 359–379.

Moody, M., Littlepage, L., and Paydar, N. (2015). Measuring social return on investment: Lessons from organizational implementation of SROI in the Netherlands and the United States. *Nonprofit Management and Leadership*, 26(1): 19–37.

Moore, M.H. (1995). *Creating Public Value: Strategic Management in Government.* Cambridge MA: Harvard University Press.

Moore, M.H. (2014). Public value accounting: Establishing the philosophical basis. *Public Administration Review*, 74(4): 465–477.

Morley, E., Vinson, E., and Hatry, H. (2001). *Outcome Measurement in Nonprofit Organizations: Current Practices and Recommendations.* Washington, DC: Urban Institute.

Mosley, J.E., and Smith, S. (2018). Human service agencies and the question of impact: Lessons for theory, policy, and practice. *Human Service Organizations: Management, Leadership, and Governance*, 42(2): 113–122.

Moulton, S. (2009). Putting together the publicness puzzle: A framework for realized publicness. *Public Administration Review*, 69(5): 889–900.

Moulton, S., and Eckerd, A. (2012). Preserving the publicness of the nonprofit sector: Resources, roles, and public values. *Nonprofit and Voluntary Sector Quarterly*, 41(4): 656–685.

Moynihan, D.P. (2005). Goal-based learning and the future of performance management. *Public Administration Review*, 65(2): 203–216.

Moynihan, D. (2014). The problem at the VA: 'performance perversity'. *LA Times*, June 1. https://www.latimes.com/opinion/op-ed/la-oe-moynihan-va-scandal-performance -perversity-20140602-story.html.

Nelson, A.A., and Gazley, B. (2014). The rise of school-supporting nonprofits. *Education Finance and Policy*, 9(4): 541–566.

Pestoff, V., Brandsen, T., and Verschuere, B. (2012). *New Public Governance, the Third Sector, and Co-Production.* New York: Routledge/Taylor & Francis.

Salamon, L.M. (1995). *Partners in Public Service: Government–Nonprofit Relations in the Modern Welfare State.* Baltimore, MD: Johns Hopkins University Press.

Schatteman, A., and Bingle, B. (2015). Philanthropy supporting government: An analysis of local library funding. *Journal of Public and Nonprofit Affairs*, 1(2): 74–86.

Skelcher, C. (2005). Public–private partnerships and hybridity. In Ewan Ferlie, Laurence Lynn Jr., and Christopher Pollitt (eds), *The Oxford Handbook of Public Management.* New York: Oxford University Press, pp. 347–368.

Seldon, S, and Sowa, J. (2004). Testing a multi-dimensional model of organizational performance: Prospects and problems. *Journal of Public Administration Research and Theory*, 14(3): 395–416.

Sowa, J., Selden, J., and Sandfort, J. (2004). No longer unmeasurable? A multidimensional integrated model of nonprofit organizational effectiveness. *Nonprofit and Voluntary Sector Quarterly*, 33(4): 711–728.

Stoker, G. (2006). Public value management: A new narrative for networked governance? *American Review of Public Administration*, 36(1): 41–57.

Thomson, D.E. (2010). Exploring the role of funders' performance reporting mandates in nonprofit performance measurement. *Nonprofit and Voluntary Sector Quarterly*, 39(4), 611–629.

US Government Accountability Office (US GAO) (2019). Watch Blog Following the Federal Dollar. https://blog.gao.gov/2019/05/28/federal-government-contracting-for-fiscal-year-2018-infographic/. Accessed October 28, 2019.

Van der Wal, Z., Nabatchi, T., and de Graaf, G. (2013). From galaxies to universe: A cross-disciplinary review and analysis of public values publications from 1969 to 2012. *American Review of Public Administration*, 45(1): 13–28.

Wolch, J. (1990). *The Shadow State: Government and Voluntary Sector in Transition*. New York: Foundation Center.

Yandle, T., Noonan, D.S., and Gazley, B. (2016). Philanthropic support of national parks: Analysis using the social-ecological systems framework. *Nonprofit and Voluntary Sector Quarterly*, 45(4): 134–155.

## 2. The challenge of nonprofit accountability and quality control in the urban hollow state: the case of public education

**Michael R. Ford**

The increased use of nonprofit providers and public–private partnerships in urban areas challenges traditional notions of public sector accountability, performance, and the very meaning of the word "public." Though the growth of what Milward and Provan (2000) deemed the hollow state was an attempt to address society's most wicked problems, the overall impact of its growth, especially in regards to accountability and increasing the population of quality organizations providing services, remains uncertain. One area where the use of nonprofit organizations to provide publicly funded services has reached scale, and raised questions of quality, is K-12 (kindergarden to 12th grade) education in the United States. Currently about 17 percent of the nonprofit sector consists of education organizations, many of which are charter and private schools providing publicly funded education via school choice programs. In Milwaukee, the focus of this study, about 40 percent of publicly funded students attend a nonprofit voucher or charter school (Ford, 2017). The city's longstanding voucher program, called the Milwaukee Parental Choice Program (MPCP), was, as of 2017, made up of 110 nonprofit schools serving almost 30 000 students. As such, the MPCP represents an excellent case for studying a full population of nonprofit entities blurring the line between private and public service delivery.

In this chapter, I use the case of the MPCP to illustrate the difficulty of creating logical effective accountability systems, and organizational-level quality control, in a hollow state enterprise. I do this by explaining the origins of urban school voucher programs, reviewing the uniqueness of the Milwaukee case and its impacts, providing a literature review on the challenge of accountability in urban hollow state arrangements, and by using a unique organizational level dataset to answer two research questions related to quality control in the urban hollow state: Were lower-performing schools more likely to fail than higher-performing schools? Did enrollment increases – that is, customer choice – mitigate the risk of organizational failure?

## THE POLICY CONTEXT: PUBLIC EDUCATION

The 1983 publication of *A Nation at Risk* (NCEE, 1983) is often cited as the impetus for the modern education reform movement. However, the challenges facing urban education systems pre-date widespread national concerns about the quality of public education in the United States. In Milwaukee, WI, for example, a 1976 federal court decision declared that the Milwaukee Public School system (MPS) was intentionally segregated (Dougherty, 2004). Other large American cities also experienced court-mandated busing aimed at deseg-regating schools. In Milwaukee, school board dysfunction, public distrust in district leadership, and intentional opaqueness about the true performance levels of district schools, served to delegitimize the MPS in the eyes of many stakeholders (Ford, 2017). The problems facing the MPS in the 1970s and 1980s however, much like the problems facing other large urban school dis-tricts, were far more complex than poor leadership or teaching quality. The problem of urban education in the 1970s and 1980s, as today, qualifies as an example of what public administration scholars deem a wicked problem (O'Toole, 1997). How so?

O'Toole (1997) describes wicked problems as those presenting "challenges that cannot be handled by dividing them up into simple pieces in near isolation from each other" (p. 46). Urban education fits O'Toole's (1997) description in several ways. First, the factors determining school success are complex and difficult to manipulate. The socioeconomic makeup of students, for example, is consistently the strongest predictor of school-level test scores. Given the compulsory nature of public education, most public schools cannot screen for students and are hence unable to manipulate the strongest predictor of school success. Factors such as spending, which in theory could be easily manip-ulated, generally do not correlate with school-level performance outcomes. Even more vexing, socioeconomic indicators such as eligibility for free and reduced-price lunch programs are mere proxies for a basket of social, health, cultural, and economic variables impacting an individual student's school performance.

Thus the problem faced by urban schools is twofold: schools have little control over who comes through the door, and generally have an incomplete picture of the specific issues students are facing outside the classroom. To that point urban schools represent a microcosm of urban society, generally serving a diverse population, but one in which low-income and minority pupils are overrepresented compared to the general population of K-12 schools. Complicating the problem of urban education is the history of desegregation orders, white flight, and funding challenges that are still very much a part of urban school systems' institutional memories (Dougherty, 2004). Urban school politics too are particularly charged, due to high levels of union influence, contentious board elections, and growing challenges to traditional school board authority (Portz et al., 1999; Howell, 2005; Hess and Leal, 2005).

There has been no shortage of strategies to address the wicked problem of education. In the 1970s activists focused on the issue of racial segregation, and multiple large urban school systems were ordered, via federal court decisions, to bus students for purposes of desegregating schools (Dougherty, 2004). However, white flight led many large urban school systems to become overwhelmingly minority, making racial integration an impossible task. In the 1980s resource inequities pushed advocates and scholars to pursue adequacy in funding as a means for improving urban education (Baker, 2016; Ravitch, 2010). Though large-scale inequities in school funding have largely been eliminated via state school funding formulas based on equity, large performance gains have not corresponded with funding increases (Greene, 2005). The 1990s and 2000s were characterized by a focus on testing, high-stakes accountability systems in which resources are tied to school performance, mayoral controlled school systems in which the traditional school board is replaced by mayoral authority, and hybrid urban school governance approaches.

The defining characteristic of hybrid urban school governance approaches is governance fragmentation, that is, the creation of alternative governance structures within the same geographic space as legacy governance structures. The legacy structures are generally the traditional public school systems overseen by a democratically elected school board. The alternative governance structures can take on many forms. In New Orleans, for example, the state of Louisiana created a Recovery School District that eventually took responsibility for a large percentage of schools formerly under the auspices of the Orleans Parish School District (Lay and Bauman, 2017). At the same time, New Orleans had a private school voucher program that allowed low-income pupils to receive publicly funded scholarships to attend private schools of their choice. Other cities, such as Cleveland, also have large private school voucher programs (EdChoice, 2017). Though New Orleans's charter schools are primarily under the authority of a single statewide school district, cities such as St Paul and Minneapolis, MN have many charter school authorizers, including universities and nonprofit organizations that are responsible for the performance of schools (Larson, 2011). Cases such as the Twin Cities reflect both macro- and micro-level governance fragmentation in that there are differences in the expectations, qualifications, and operational models deployed across governing boards overseeing different types of urban schools and systems.

The reality of governance fragmentation in urban education presents many difficult-to-address questions. At the macro level, who should be held accountable for the performance of K-12 education systems? Who is in charge of setting education policy? Who defines macro-level goals for an urban education system? How is school-level quality control implemented? At the school governing board level, how should boards be structured? What constituencies should be represented on governing boards? To whom should governing boards be accountable? To what extent does public funding translate into the expectation for governing transparency? As I argue in previous work (Ford, 2017), none of these questions can be easily answered, but they nonetheless represent the challenge of creating successful quality control mechanisms for organizations operating in fragmented hollow state governing environments. In the following section I provide details about the case of Milwaukee, WI, a city that went all in on the hybrid urban school governance approach as a means for addressing the wicked problem of urban education.

**Voucher Policy in Milwaukee**

The MPCP began in 1990 as the first limited experiment in giving low-income children a government-funded voucher to attend the private school of their choice. Though the concept of school vouchers is grounded in Milton Friedman's (1955) calls for a free-market approach to public education, the MPCP was always, and still is, a restricted program falling short of Friedman's vision. Initially, the MPCP was limited to just seven non-sectarian schools required to enroll less than 50 percent of their students through the MPCP (Ford, 2017; Witte, 2000). Though the MPCP evolved steadily over time, eventually allowing religious schools, increasing family household income limits from 175 percent to 300 percent of the federal poverty level, and being subject to steadily increasing school-level regulation and testing requirements, the basic idea of voucher policy remained consistent. Parents pick a participating school of their choice, apply directly to that school, are screened to ensure they meet income requirements and are City of Milwaukee residents, and are admitted. If a school receives more application than there are seats, a random lottery must be conducted. Once a student is enrolled, a school receives a payment worth the lesser of the school's actual audited per-pupil cost, or the maximum allowable voucher payment ($7530 for a K-8 student and $8176 for a high school student in 2017–2018).

As can be seen in Figure 2.1, enrollment in the MPCP has grown steadily over time, both in raw numbers as well as in relation to student enrollment in MPS. As the MPCP grew it attracted significant attention in the education and public management literatures. Generally, the MPCP has been shown to have a modest positive academic impact on voucher user test scores and attainment (Witte et al., 2014; Cowen et al., 2013; Ford and Andersson, 2019). Hoxby (2003), Greene and Marsh (2009), Chakrabarti (2008), and Carnoy et al. (2007) explored the competitive effects of Milwaukee's school voucher policy on public school students, finding small but measurable public school performance gains attributable to competition from the MPCP. Ford (2011), Ford and Andersson (2016) and Flanders (2018) explored the organizational lifespans of MPCP schools, finding the MPCP created significant entrepreneurial activity, but also a large number of school failures. Finally, Cowen et al. (2012) found voucher users to be a highly mobile population, showing significant mobility between Milwaukee's school sectors.

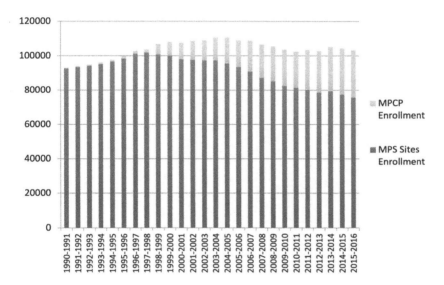

*Figure 2.1     Milwaukee public schools and Milwaukee Parental Choice Program enrollment history*

Overall, the research consensus on the MPCP is that the program offers significant but substantively small academic benefits, and creates many externalities such as school closures and mobility that were not considered at the time of the program's creation (Ford and Andersson, 2019). However, as I conclude in previous work (Ford, 2017), the MPCP is large and important enough that it is a permanent part of Milwaukee's education infrastructure. Positive improvement in the overall quality of Milwaukee's education system is impossible without engagement with MPCP schools. Figure 2.2 displays the extent to which public education is fragmented in Milwaukee today. As can be seen, data from 2016–2017 indicate that only 57 percent of publicly funded students in Milwaukee are attending a traditional MPS public school. Fourteen percent of pupils attend non-union charter schools authorized by the MPS, the City of Milwaukee, and the University of Wisconsin-Milwaukee; 6 percent attend suburban schools via Wisconsin's public school choice programs; and 23 percent attend a private school via the MPCP. As mentioned earlier, the reality in Milwaukee can be described as a hybrid approach to urban school governance in which there are multiple competing systems operating under different governance structures, different funding models, and different levels of regulation. Despite their differences, their customer bases (student demographics), and performance levels (test scores), are remarkably similar.

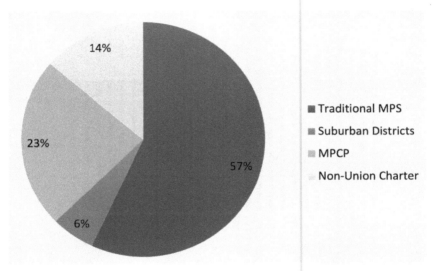

14%

23%

57%

6%

■ Traditional MPS

■ Suburban Districts

▨ MPCP

    Non-Union Charter

*Figure 2.2      Distribution of publicly funded Milwaukee pupils, 2016–2017*

Milwaukee's persistent low test scores relative to both other Wisconsin districts and other large urban school districts indicates that Milwaukee's voucher experience has not adequately addressed the wicked problem of urban education in the city (NCES, 2011). But, Milwaukee's experience does provide a fascinating test of hollow state theory in the area of quality control. In the following sections I review the literature on public sector accountability in the context of network governance and hollow state theory, present data relating to quality control in the MPCP, and test two hypotheses regarding quality control in the urban hollow state.

## WHAT WE KNOW

Romzek and Dubnick (1987) used the case of the Challenger disaster to create a widely used taxonomy of public sector accountability. There are, Romzek and Dubnick (1987) conclude, four different overlapping accountability types in the public sector. There is legal accountability, which is characterized by high levels of external control; bureaucratic accountability, which is characterized by high levels of internal control; political accountability, which is characterized by low levels of external control; and professional accountability, which is characterized by low levels of internal control. In the traditional school district context legal accountability would be state laws regulating district operations; bureaucratic accountability would be internal district policies and established modes of communication created by the superintendent; political accountability would come in the form of the democratically elected school board; while professional accountability could refer to the teaching profession and the unions and professional associations of which teachers are a part. Though the application of accountability is made difficult by the overlapping nature of accountability types, the descriptive power of the taxonomy is relatively straightforward and stable in traditional public sector service arrangements. In a school district, for example, the school board serves as the democratically elected governance body linking the values of citizens to the operations of the school district. Citizens dissatisfied with the performance of their public education system can implement accountability by voting their school board representative out of office (Lutz and Iannaccone, 2008). However, the explanatory value of Romzek and Dubnick's (1987) taxonomy and the straightforward nature of accountability in traditional bureaucratic systems are problematized by hollow state arrangements.

The hollow state refers to "the devolution of power and decentralization of services from central government to subnational government and, by extension, to third parties," such as nonprofit organizations (Milward and Provan, 2003, p. 2). In other words, the hollow state is created when the responsibility for traditional public service delivery is shifted from a single central government provider to a decentralized network of public and nonprofit organizations (Provan and Milward, 2001). The reasons behind the growth of the hollow state are rooted in theories of new public management, which state that government performance and efficiency can be improved when market forces are introduced to traditionally monopolistic government activities (Kettl, 2005). Peters and Pierre (1998) refer to the managing of this new paradigm as governance. Though the very idea of governance has its critics (see Stillman, 1999; Frederickson et al., 2012), high-profile and high-cost services such as public education are increasingly provided by decentralized networks, making the understanding of governance essential to understanding modern public administration.

DeLeon (1998) speaks to the challenge of creating accountable governance arrangements when "goals are unclear or conflicting" and "there is no agreement on what results should be obtained" (p. 551). Such is the accountability conundrum facing Milwaukee education, where common goals for the system as a whole have never been clearly articulated; and even if they could be articulated, there is no agreed-upon entity to voice said common goal (Ford, 2017). Thus the question posed by DeLeon (1998) and illustrated by the Milwaukee education experience is not just how to hold diffused organizations accountable, but what accountability in the hollow state even means. Milward and Provan (2000) argue that accountability in the hollow state requires a principal–agent relationship so that some recognized entity is able to articulate and impose accountability on actual service providers. The Wisconsin Department of Public Instruction (DPI) operates as somewhat of a principal in the Milwaukee voucher case, but the relationship is not nearly as clear as suggested by Milward and Provan (2000). Whitaker et al. (2004) advocate accountability as a collaborative approach where government entities facilitate the success of hollow state actors as opposed to policing their compliance failures, but as will be demonstrated, this approach is not present in Milwaukee.

Perhaps most relevant to the Milwaukee voucher case is the work of Willems and Van Dooren (2011), who conclude that private–public partnerships can create an accountability paradox where the burden of accountability for individual nonprofit organizations providing government services appears to increase despite the fact that macro-level accountability for the quality of services provided is static or even decreasing. In other words, accountability as traditionally understood for organizations can increase even if the hollow state network as a whole is not accountable for its performance. Such is the case in Milwaukee: Ford and Andersson (2016) demonstrate that the level of accountability placed on individual voucher schools has increased steadily since 1990, but that the overall performance of Milwaukee's publicly funded education system remains stagnant with no clear signs of progress. To put it another way, though individual organizations in Milwaukee face steadily increasing regulatory requirements, the system as a whole is not being held accountable for its performance.

The unit of analysis in this article is the MPCP schools themselves. So what exactly does accountability look like for MPCP schools? To whom are MPCP schools accountable, and for what are they accountable (Bardach and Lesser, 1996)? First, MPCP schools face fiscal accountability measures in the form of having to file an annual audit, being required to return any state overpayments for accepted students who do not actually enroll, undergo mandatory financial training, and ensure their audit does not show evidence of an ongoing concern.

Under Wisconsin state statute, the DPI can terminate schools from the voucher program for failing to comply with these fiscal measures. Because MPCP schools are on average about 80 percent reliant on voucher revenues (see Ford, 2017), no schools terminated from the voucher program have continued to exist as private schools. Hence, in practice, termination from the MPCP is akin to shutting down the organization. Second, DPI can terminate schools that pose an imminent health or safety threat to pupils as determined by DPI's elected state superintendent. Third, MPCP schools can be terminated for failing to meet private school requirements pre-dating the MPCP, regarding hours of instruction and the presence of a sequentially progressive curriculum. Fourth, MPCP schools can be terminated by DPI if they fail to obtain and or/maintain a third-party accreditation. Fifth, schools can be held accountable by parents; if enrollments drop and parents vote with their feet, schools will eventually fail (Ford and Andersson, 2016). Interestingly, performance is absent from the list of accountability measures. Though all MPCP schools are required to administer the official state test and to release school-level results, there is no mechanism for DPI to terminate a school for its academic performance. Indeed, there are several MPCP schools that, according to official DPI test scores results, boast few if any students deemed proficient in math and reading. Though parental accountability, fiscal accountability, and third-party accreditation could all arguably serve as proxies for academic achievement, in practice low-performing schools continue to enroll large numbers of MPCP pupils.

Over the life of the program the five modes of accountability have been frequently exercised. Ford and Andersson (2016) found that 42 percent of all voucher schools failed in the city, concluding that start-up schools were at particularly elevated risk for being shut down by DPI, or closing voluntarily. Due to the absence of school-level performance data over the life of the MPCP, Ford and Andersson (2016) were unable to use test school performance as a determinant. Recently, Flanders (2018) built upon Ford and Andersson's study by conducting a survival analysis for MPCP schools for the years in which testing data were available, and found schools with lower science and social studies scores were most likely to close. Flanders (2018) created an eight-point scale to measure social studies and science scores, however, rather than the more generally accepted use of proficiency levels (ranging from 0 to 100) in reading and math. Flanders (2018) also failed to take into account whether a school was a start-up; that is, whether it existed prior to accepting voucher money, which was determined by Ford and Andersson (2016) to substantially increase failure risk.

In this analysis I use MPCP data from 2010 to 2014, the only four years in which participating schools administered a common test, to test the link between school performance proficiency levels in math and reading and school closure, and school enrollment growth and school closure risk. Specifically,

I expect that higher-performing schools, and those with higher growth rates, were comparably less likely to have closed.

## DATA AND METHODOLOGICAL APPROACH

I test the two hypotheses using a unique unbalanced panel dataset populated with school-level performance, demographic, enrollment, and fiscal data for the years 2010 to 2014. Summary statistics for all variables are presented in Tables 2.1 and 2.2. In Table 2.1, the *Pct. Proficient Reading* variables refer to the percentage of pupils within a school who were deemed proficient or advanced on the Wisconsin Knowledge and Concepts Exam (WKCE) in any given year. The *Year in Program* variable was created by the author to determine each school's year of participation in the MPCP. *Fundraising Per-Pupil* indicates the difference between the school's actual audited per-pupil cost, and the maximum voucher amount. By definition, all funding of a school's per-pupil cost above the maximum voucher amount must be obtained from fundraising. The *Pct. Voucher* variable indicates the percentage of students within a school attending via a voucher, while *Enrollment* refers to the school's total enrollment in each year. Finally, *Annual Growth* is simply the difference between a school's enrollment from one year to the next. The categorical variables displayed in Table 2.2 include the dependent variables, *Still in Program*, *Terminated*, and *Market Exit*. *Still in Program* simply means a school did not exit the MPCP that year. *Terminated* means a school was closed by DPI that year, while *Market Exit* means a school closed voluntarily in any given year. *Catholic*, *Lutheran*, *Other Christian*, and *Non-Sectarian* refers to the religious affiliation of schools, while *Start-Up* indicates that a school opened specifically for the purposes of accessing voucher revenues; that is, it never operated without government funding.

*Table 2.1      Summary statistics for continuous variables*

|  | N | Mean | Std Dev. |
|---|---|---|---|
| *Pct. Proficient Reading* | 384 | 12.53 | 12.92 |
| *Pct. Proficient Math* | 384 | 14.1 | 14.75 |
| *Year in Program* | 409 | 10.14 | 4.89 |
| *Fundraising Per-Pupil* | 409 | 1197.95 | 1197.95 |
| *Pct. Voucher* | 409 | 83.97 | 24.77 |
| *Enrollment* | 409 | 228.36 | 233.78 |
| *Annual Growth* | 376 | 16.86 | 56.12 |

I first test my hypotheses using four separate Cox regression models in which *Closure* is the dependent variable, *School* is the ID, and *Year in Program* is the time variable. Conceptually, the Cox regression method measures the relationship between each of the independent variables over the four years in question, and the cumulative risk of a school failure. I then present two separate multinomial logistic regression models predicting the likelihood of a school being terminated by the DPI, or closing voluntarily, against the base outcome of remaining in the MPCP. Because I am using panel data consisting of multiple schools across multiple years, I cluster the standard errors by school. Note that a total of 121 schools are included in the panel dataset.

*Table 2.2    Summary statistics for categorical variables*

|  | Yes | No |
|---|---|---|
| *Still in Program* | 393 | 15 |
| *Terminated* | 8 | 400 |
| *Market Exit* | 7 | 401 |
| *Catholic* | 127 | 282 |
| *Lutheran* | 115 | 294 |
| *Other Christian* | 85 | 324 |
| *Non-Sectarian* | 64 | 345 |
| *Start-Up* | 125 | 284 |

## STUDY RESULTS AND NEW INSIGHTS

The results of the survival analysis predicting school closure are displayed in Table 2.3. Model 1 indicates no statistically significant relationship between reading proficiency levels and risk of school closure. Consistent with previous research, there is a relationship between start-up status and closure risk, as well as enrollment and reduced closure risk. Model 2 shows no significant relationship between reading proficiency and reduced failure risk; however, schools with growing enrollments do significantly reduce their closure risk. A similar pattern emerges in Models 3 and 4, in which there are no significant relationships between math proficiency and closure risk; however, there are relationships between total school enrollment, start-up status, annual growth, and reduced closure risk. Note that in Models 2 and 4, schools for which there are no observations in the previous year are excluded because calculation of a growth variable was impossible.

*Table 2.3*     *Survival analysis predicting school closure*

| Variables | (Model 1) Closure | (Model 2) Closure | (Model 3) Closure | (Model 4) Closure |
|---|---|---|---|---|
| *Pct. Proficient Reading* | -0.0594 | -0.0492 | | |
| | (0.0480) | (0.0471) | | |
| *Pct. Proficient Math* | | | -0.0285 | -0.0169 |
| | | | (0.0358) | (0.0356) |
| *Pct. Voucher* | -0.0114 | -0.0126 | -0.0119 | -0.0120 |
| | (0.0168) | (0.0180) | (0.0173) | (0.0193) |
| *Fundraising Per-Pupil* | -0.000376 | -0.000372 | -0.000371 | -0.000359 |
| | (0.000341) | (0.000361) | (0.000331) | (0.000358) |
| *Catholic* | -0.0664 | 0.713 | -0.0881 | 0.466 |
| | (1.447) | (1.575) | (1.458) | (1.586) |
| *Lutheran* | 0.766 | 1.348 | 0.901 | 1.397 |
| | (1.250) | (1.415) | (1.208) | (1.385) |
| *Other Christian* | -0.0471 | 0.300 | 0.000340 | 0.339 |
| | (0.633) | (0.703) | (0.641) | (0.709) |
| *Enrollment* | -0.0131*** | -0.0155*** | -0.0132*** | -0.0154*** |
| | (0.00471) | (0.00560) | (0.00479) | (0.00561) |
| *Start-Up* | 1.918* | 1.786 | 2.253** | 2.007* |
| | (1.049) | (1.149) | (0.991) | (1.100) |
| *Annual Growth* | | -0.0139** | | -0.0149** |
| | | (0.00619) | | (0.00625) |
| | | | | |
| Observations | 384 | 358 | 384 | 358 |

*Notes:* Standard errors in parentheses. *** $p < 0.01$, ** $p < 0.05$, * $p < 0.1$.

The results of the survival analysis displayed in Table 2.2 do not support hypothesis one: there is no evidence of a link between math and reading proficiency levels and closure risk. There is support for hypothesis two, as schools with comparably larger growth rates face a reduced closure risk. Table 2.4 displays the results of two multinomial logistic regression models predicting the likelihood that a school is terminated from the MPCP by the DPI, or closes of its own accord, compared to remaining in the MPCP. As mentioned, robust standards errors are clustered by each of the 121 schools in the two models. Model 5 indicates that schools with higher percentages of students proficient in reading are comparably less likely to be terminated from the MPCP. There is no relationship between reading proficiency and the likelihood of a market exit, nor a relationship between math proficiency and the likelihood of any mode of exit. Like the survival models, there is a statistically significant relationship between school size and reduced closure risk. There is also a significant relationship between being a start-up school and higher likelihood of being terminated by the DPI. Finally, religious affiliation generally decreases closure risk, while fundraising decreases likelihood of termination.

*Table 2.4*     *Multinomial logit predicting school closure*

|  | (Model 5) | | (Model 6) | |
| --- | --- | --- | --- | --- |
| Variables | Terminated | Market exit | Terminated | Market exit |
| *Pct. Proficient Reading* | -0.182** | -0.0588 | | |
|  | (0.0887) | (0.0578) | | |
| *Pct. Proficient Math* | | | -0.0179 | -0.0633 |
|  | | | (0.109) | (0.0633) |
| *Year in Program* | 0.0545 | 0.102 | 0.0224 | 0.100 |
|  | (0.105) | (0.101) | (0.0978) | (0.106) |
| *Fundraising Per-Pupil* | -0.00356* | -7.13e-05 | -0.00347* | -7.47e-05 |
|  | (0.00203) | (0.000201) | (0.00198) | (0.000224) |
| *Pct. Voucher* | -0.115*** | -0.0319** | -0.113*** | -0.0321** |
|  | (0.0343) | (0.0150) | (0.0405) | (0.0156) |
| *Catholic* | -17.07*** | -1.249 | -16.77*** | -0.780 |
|  | (1.450) | (1.162) | (1.663) | (1.410) |
| *Lutheran* | -17.45*** | -0.397 | -17.73*** | 0.0341 |
|  | (1.364) | (0.885) | (2.161) | (1.034) |
| *Other Christian* | 0.211 | -18.57*** | -0.0725 | -18.15*** |
|  | (0.909) | (0.721) | (0.824) | (0.818) |
| *Start-Up* | 2.428* | 0.331 | 4.784* | 0.635 |
|  | (1.262) | (0.985) | (2.740) | (0.787) |
| *Enrollment* | -0.0207*** | -0.00654** | -0.0212*** | -0.00607* |
|  | (0.00680) | (0.00330) | (0.00649) | (0.00325) |
| *Constant* | 9.326*** | 0.173 | 6.979* | -0.215 |
|  | (3.233) | (1.352) | (3.857) | (1.305) |
|  | | | | |
| Observations | 383 | 383 | 383 | 383 |

*Notes:* Robust standard errors in parentheses clustered by school. *** p < 0.01, ** p < 0.05, * p < 0.1.

Models 5 and 6, like Models 1 through 4, show very little evidence of a strong relationship between academic proficiency and the modes of accountability implemented in the MPCP. Rather, variables independent of formal account-ability mechanisms – that is, school size – demonstrated that ability to exist without voucher revenues, and attraction of students as measured via annual growth, best mitigate closure risk.

## IMPLICATIONS AND LESSONS LEARNED

On the surface these findings are not terribly surprising, but are somewhat concerning in regard to effectively implementing accountability in the urban hollow state. How so? The quixotic MPCP accountability framework seems to be effective in holding organizationally weak schools to account. Schools that have reached economies of scale, that have the ability to attract increasing numbers of students (and hence voucher revenues), that have established track records independent of the voucher program, and that are affiliated with religious umbrella institutions, are unlikely to be held accountable via closure. Yet, the same accountability framework that favors stable name-brand schools does not reward or punish academic performance. Simply, the many proxy variables for organizational strength around which the MPCP account-ability framework evolved do not appear tied to actual student performance within schools. The situation in Milwaukee's voucher sector presents its own accountability paradox (Willems and Van Dooren, 2011). Schools are being held accountable via the ultimate consequence of closure (see Kaufman, 1991), but are not being held accountable for the very thing needed to address the wicked problem of urban education: performance gains.

Milwaukee education's accountability paradox offers many lessons for urban hollow state service-delivery arrangements. First, it illustrates just how difficult it is to create effective accountability systems when using nonprofit organizations to provide public services at scale. MPCP schools are still inde-pendent nonprofits despite their overwhelming dependence on government funds; as such there is a distance between organizational accountability and system accountability that does not exist in traditional public centralized bureaucracies. Though state regulators created various accountability meas-ures over time, accountability for system performance as a whole failed to materialize. Instead, accountability took the form of transparency measures divorced from quality measures, and the blunt instrument of organizational closure.

Second, and related to this, the MPCP illustrates the flaws in the "stick" approach to hollow state accountability. As demonstrated, the MPCP's regu-latory framework is quite adept at closing down nonprofit organizations, but there is no clear link between organizational performance levels and likelihood of closure. It is true that most shuttered organizations were weak in terms of their finances and/or management, but that does not negate the fact that schools with stronger finances and management are nonetheless performing at low levels. Thus, when attempting to bring nonprofit service delivery systems up to scale there is a need to consider incentivizing approaches to accountability that encourage and reward performance, not just punish organizational weakness.

Third, though the MPCP could certainly fit into the framework of government failure theory, the fact that the nonprofits tasked with addressing the government failure are performing at similarly low levels demonstrates that it cannot be assumed that decentralized systems of nonprofit sector organizations will outperform centralized government bureaucracies. It follows that the performance of hollow state governance systems are dependent on the performance of organizations operating within them. The MPCP is an urban governance reform designed to improve the overall service delivery of public education in the City of Milwaukee by interjecting competition through new and existing nonprofit providers. In practice the decentralized system of MPCP schools mirrors, in both clientele and performance (see Ford, 2017), the public system it was designed to reform.

Fourth, this analysis reveals that organizational quality does not necessarily equal higher performance levels when nonprofits are dealing with society's wicked problems. Though the case of the MPCP represents just one population of nonprofit organizations working in one specific service area, the fact that the MPCP is subject to a system of externally accepted testing measures provides a unique opportunity to objectively measure nonprofit performance outcomes. The results indicate that organizational strength and stability is not always an effective proxy for performance. There is a population of low-performing schools in Milwaukee that are organizationally stable and could be considered "successful" via fiscal and structural systems indicators.

The overall lesson from Milwaukee's voucher experience? Accountability for nonprofit organizations in the urban hollow state must be explicitly performance-driven in order to be effective. A voucher-driven approach in particular introduces the tragedy of the commons problem, where what is best for the individual may not be best for society. In the Milwaukee voucher case, for example, there have been consistently high levels of parental satisfaction with the MPCP, despite overall middling academic effects. The incongruence is likely a result of the differing incentives for nonprofits and public organization. A nonprofit voucher school is dependent on customer satisfaction for funding, wheareas a public organization is dependent on a more complex web of legislative oversight for funding. To put it another way, a voucher school may meet the goals of the parent without meeting the broader goals of a public education system. While this is not problematic for a strictly private school, a school that is publicly funded should logically expect some level of oversight tied to broader societal goals. As demonstrated, this requires a deliberate approach to performance-based accountability.

But how can a performance-based approach happen? It is particularly challenging for nonprofit schools funded by voucher, as the public managers administering the program are completely divorced from the actual organizational structures running schools. Thus, there is a classic hollow state governance problem where public managers must manage quality for a service over which they have no direct control. However, it is possible for a voucher-style program to create public value when used at scale. Citizen satisfaction, though not always aligned with broader societal goals, is nonetheless a positive outcome. Vouchers are innovative in that they allow for individual expression of policy preferences, which can lead to the aforementioned citizen satisfaction, but also can signal to policymakers what types of programming citizens desire. Vouchers are an innovative mechanism for grass-roots-driven government, but as a mechanism they are not inherently good or bad. To put it another way, the quality of a voucher-driven reform is a function of the quality of the organizations enabled by the reform.

Thus, the challenge for policymakers and public managers alike is to capitalize on the potential of voucher-driven innovation without sacrificing overall quality and accountability. One potential way to accomplish this balancing act is a meta-governance strategy in which an independent board or body articulates goals and imposes a degree of order and control over nonprofit organizations that choose to take public money (Peters, 2010). A possible alternative would be a government body that serves a similar function; however, such boards risk simply reproducing a centralized bureaucracy composed of highly regulated nonprofit organizations. More research on urban hollow state governance arrangements, especially in areas outside of education, would help bring the generalizability of Milwaukee's lessons into focus. Nonetheless, the presented data and analysis illustrate the difficulty of holding nonprofit organizations accountable in the urban hollow state.

## REFERENCES

Baker, B.D. (2016). *Does Money Matter in Education?* Washington, DC: Albert Shanker Institute.

Bardach, E., and Lesser, C. (1996). Accountability in human services collaboratives— For what? and to whom? *Journal of Public Administration Research and Theory*, 6(2), 197–224.

Carnoy, M., Adamson, F., Chudgar, A., Luschei, T., and Witte, J. (2007). *Vouchers and Public School Performance*. Washington, DC: Economic Policy Institute.

Chakrabarti, R. (2008). Can increasing private school participation and monetary loss in a voucher program affect public school performance? Evidence from Milwaukee. *Journal of Public Economics, 92*, 1371–1393.

Cowen, J.M., Fleming, D.J., Witte, J.F., and Wolf, P.J. (2012). Going public: Who leaves a large, longstanding, and widely available urban voucher program? *American Educational Research Journal, 49*(2), 231–256.

Cowen, J.M., Fleming, D.J., Witte, J.F., Wolf, P.J., and Kisida, B. (2013). School vouchers and student attainment: Evidence from a state-mandated study of Milwaukee's Parental Choice Program. *Policy Studies Journal, 41*(1), 147–168.

DeLeon, L. (1998). Accountability in a "reinvented" government. *Public Administration, 76*(3), 539–558.

Dougherty, J. (2004). *More Than One Struggle: The Evolution of Black School Reform in Milwaukee.* Chapel Hill, NC: University of North Carolina Press.

EdChoice (2017). *The ABCs of School Choice.* Indianapolis, IN: EdChoice.

Flanders, W.D. (2018). The benefit of churn? Examining the market characteristics of the Milwaukee Parental Choice Program. *Journal of School Choice, 12*(2), 254–270.

Ford, M. (2011). School exits in the Milwaukee Parental Choice Program: Evidence of a marketplace? *Journal of School Choice, 5*(2), 182–204.

Ford, M.R. (2017). *The Consequences of Governance Fragmentation.* Lanham, MD: Lexington Books.

Ford, M.R., and Andersson, F.O. (2016). Determinants of organizational failure in the Milwaukee school voucher program. *Policy Studies Journal.* doi:10.1111/psj.12164.

Ford, M.R., and Andersson, F.O. (2019). Taking stock and moving forward: Lessons from two plus decades of research on the Milwaukee Parental Choice Program. *Journal of School Choice, 13*(2), 158–176.

Frederickson, H.G., Smith, K.B., Larimer, C.W., and Licari, M.J. (2012). *The Public Administration Theory Primer.* Boulder, CO: Westview Press.

Friedman, M. (1955). The role of government in public education. In R.A. Solow (ed.), *Economics and the Public Interest* (pp. 123–144). New Brunswick, NY: Rutgers Press.

Greene, J.P. (2005). *Education Myths: What Special Interest Groups Want You to Believe About Our Schools—And Why It Isn't So.* Lanham, MD: Rowman & Littlefield Publishers.

Greene, J.P., and Marsh, R.H. (2009). *The Effect of Milwaukee's Parental Choice Program on Student Achievement in Milwaukee Public Schools.* Fayetteville, AR: School Choice Demonstration Project, University of Arkansas.

Hess, F., and Leal, D. (2005). School house politics: Expenditures, interests, and competition in school board elections. In W.G. Howell (ed.), *Besieged: School Boards and the Future of Education Politics* (pp. 228–253). Washington DC: Brookings Institution Press.

Howell, W.G. (Ed.) (2005). *Besieged: School Boards and the Future of Education Politics.* Washington DC: Brookings Institution Press.

Hoxby, C.M. (2003). School choice and school competition: Evidence from the United States. *Swedish Economic Policy Review, 10*(2), 11–67.

Kaufman, H. (1991). *Time, Chance, and Organizations: Natural Selection in a Perilous Environment.* New York: Chatham House Publishers.

Kettl, D.F. (2005). *The Global Public Management Revolution* (2nd edn). Washington, DC: Brookings Institution Press.

Larson, L. (2011). Minnesota's Charter School Law. St Paul, MN: Research Department of the Minnesota House of Representatives.

Lay, J.C., and Bauman, A. (2017). Private governance of public schools: Representation, priorities, and compliance in New Orleans charter school boards. *Urban Affairs Review,* 1078087417748783.

Lutz, F.W., and Iannoccone, L. (2008). The dissatisfaction theory of American democracy. In T.L. Asbury (ed.), *The Future of School Board Governance* (pp. 3–24). Lanham, MD: Roman & Littlefield.

Milward, H.B., and Provan, K.G. (2000). Governing the hollow state. *Journal of Public Administration and Theory*, *10*(2), 359–379.

Milward, H.B., and Provan, K. (2003). Managing the hollow state: Collaboration and contracting. *Public Management Review*, *5*(1), 1–18.

National Center for Education Statistics (NCES) (2011). *The Nation's Report Card: Trial Urban District Assessment Mathematics 2011*. Washington, DC: US Department of Education.

National Commission on Excellence in Education (NCEE) (1983). A nation at risk: The imperative for educational reform. *Elementary School Journal*, *84*(2), 113–130.

O'Toole Jr, L.J. (1997). Treating networks seriously: Practical and research-based agendas in public administration. *Public Administration Review*, *57*(1), 45–52.

Peters, B.G. (2010). Meta-governance and public management. In S.P. Osborne (ed.), *The New Public Governance* (pp. 36–51). New York: Routledge.

Peters, B.G., and Pierre, J. (1998). Governance without government? Rethinking public administration. *Journal of Public Administration Research and Theory*, *8*(2), 223–243.

Portz, J., Stein, L., and Jones, R.R. (1999). *City Schools and City Politics*. Lawrence, KS: University Press of Kansas.

Provan, K.G., and Milward, H.B. (2001). Do networks really work? A framework for evaluating public-sector organizational networks. *Public Administration Review*, *61*(4), 414–423.

Ravitch, D. (2010). *The Life and Death of the Great American School System: How Testing and Choice are Undermining Education*. New York: Basic Books.

Romzek, B.S., and Dubnick, M.J. (1987). Accountability in the public sector: Lessons from the Challenger tragedy. *Public Administration Review*, *47*(3), 227–238.

Stillman, R.J. (1999). *Preface to Public Administration* (2nd edn). Burke, VA: Chatelaine Press.

Whitaker, G.P., Altman-Sauer, L., and Henderson, M. (2004). Mutual accountability between governments and nonprofits: moving beyond "surveillance" to "service." *American Review of Public Administration*, *34*(2), 115–133.

Willems, T., and Van Dooren, W. (2011). Lost in diffusion? How collaborative arrangements lead to an accountability paradox. *International Review of Administrative Sciences*, *77*(3), 505–530.

Witte, J.F. (2000). *The Market Approach to Education: An Analysis of America's First Voucher Program*. Princeton, NJ: Princeton University Press.

Witte, J.F., Wolf, P.J., Cowen, J.M., Carlson, D.E., and Fleming, D.J. (2014). High-stakes choice achievement and accountability in the nation's oldest urban voucher program. *Educational Evaluation and Policy Analysis*. DOI: 0162373714534521.

# 3. Are outsourced public health services linked to better health outcomes? Findings from a national study of service contracting by local health departments

**Tianshu Zhao and Kelly LeRoux**

One policy arena in which hollow state actors have played an increasingly important role in delivering needed public services is health care. Driven by new public management and government reinvention principles, contracting out for many types of public services, including health care, has become commonplace, particularly at the local level where fiscally constrained municipalities and counties have sought ways to keep up with increasing service demands and complex public health needs in the face of declining resources.

Theories of contracting suggest that competition injected into the public services market will lead to greater efficiency and effectiveness, as private firms are forced by market pressures to provide high-quality services, and demonstrate their value in the marketplace of prospective buyers. Many studies within the contracting literature concentrate on the efficiency question: whether contracting reduces or contains costs. Fewer studies, however, have endeavored to examine the effectiveness question: whether contracting out public services to private organizations enhances service quality. In this chapter we examine the link between local public health departments' (LHDs) decision to contract out for health services, and a set of corresponding community health outcomes. This is a topic that has yet to be explored in the public sector contracting literature.

## THE POLICY CONTEXT: PUBLIC HEALTH

Public health provides an excellent context in which to study the implications of contracting. In the United States in recent years, health services have been increasingly shifted from states to local-level governments including counties, cities, and townships where they are funded predominantly by federal and state funds. Every day, approximately 2800 local health departments (LHDs) act as the front lines of the United States (US) public health system to promote and protect the health and well-being for all people in their communities where they live, learn, work, and play; ensure the safety of water and food; prevent communicable diseases; take action on emergencies; and promote wellness by encouraging healthy behaviors (American Public Health Association, 2019; National Association of County and City Health Officials, 2017b).

Whereas LHDs undertake overall responsibility to promote population health, they are confronted with complex social and behavioral problems, expanded population health needs, rapid disease transmission across national boundaries, fiscal constraints, budget pressure, and diminished capacity (Reich, 2002). In the past decade, the economic downturn resulted in a deteriorated tax base for state and county general revenue. In the meanwhile, the implementation of the Affordable Care Act created more complexity for LHDs. Those problems, pressures, and challenges created incentives for LHDs to both conserve costs and promote service quality. Such an environment promoted a variety of solutions, including contracting out more health services to for-profit and nonprofit organizations as well as other government agencies (Issel et al., 2015).

Although some privatization theorists argue that the private sector can deliver public goods and services more efficiently and effectively than the public sector, others contend that certain services such as public health should not be contracted (Keane et al., 2002). Contracting out is successful in some locales but the idea is met with reluctance in other places. There is not always sufficient evidence to confirm whether contracting out will achieve public goals of improved service quality. Are outsourced services by local health departments linked to better public health outcomes? How effective are contracting out practices in local health departments?

In this chapter, we address these questions through a national study of contracting by local health departments, using data from National Profile of Local Health Department Study, combined with county-level health outcome data from the County Health Rankings and Roadmaps (CHRR). These data, paired with various controls for community health outcomes, allow us to examine whether public sector contracting by local public health departments is linked to better health outcomes at the community level on four specific health issues: frequent mental distress, sexually transmitted infections, teen births, and adult smoking. We find that contracting out for some public health functions is indeed linked to improved health outcomes, but only for some types of services. When services with lower transaction costs (lower asset specificity and easier service measurability) are contracted out, we see a positive effect on corresponding community health outcomes.

In the next section, we review major theories and previous empirical research relevant to public sector collaboration and effectiveness. Next, we develop the theoretical framework for understanding the relationship between characteristics of services and health outcomes. We then describe our data, measures, and methods of analysis. Next we interpret our results and conclude with a discussion of their implications for managing hollow state health care actors.

## WHAT WE KNOW

### Contracting Activities and Outcomes

A number of empirical studies have examined the outcomes of contracting activities in federal, state, and local public agencies from the perspectives of accountability, efficiency, effectiveness, and responsiveness. The majority of studies focused on the consequences of contracting are concerned with the efficiency question, otherwise described as cost savings or economizing benefits of outsourcing. Public choice theory suggests that public agencies have monopoly power in delivering public goods and services, which results in oversupply and inefficiency . The solution proposed by public choice theory is to replace monopoly with competition in public service markets. In the presence of competition, public agencies contracting for services should result in improved efficiency—cost savings or lower spending—for those services produced by external providers . Boyne (1998a) summarizes empirical evidence and suggests that "production by a private firm appears to lead to lower spending and higher efficiency in the fire service, highway construction and maintenance, property maintenance, and janitorial services" (p. 479). Savas (2000) examined contracting practices in California, New Jersey, and New York, as well as in other countries, and demonstrated that public officials were satisfied with the cost savings. Hodge's (2000) international review of privatization performance also exhibits cost savings through outsourcing. Brudney et al. (2005), on the other hand, find that only one-third of state agencies in their analysis reported service cost savings as a result of contracting.

In contrast to the many studies that focus on efficiency gains, there are few empirical studies that demonstrate the impact of outsourcing on service delivery effectiveness or service quality . As O'Toole and Meier have pointed out, "The evidence on contracting is complex but suggests the possibility of cost savings, at least under some circumstances. Much less frequently examined, however, is the related question of service quality, despite the fact that the theoretical arguments also tout the prospect of positive impacts here" (O'Toole and Meier, 2004, p. 342). Romzek and Johnston (2005) contend that the reasons for this may include: (1) it is hard for contractors to control and measure outcomes; (2) there are disagreements about performance standards; and (3) there is a time lag between the program intervention and the desired outcomes.

The limited research on service contracting quality outcomes points to mixed results. Examining contracting in the context of public schools, O'Toole and Meier (2004, p. 344) conclude that it can improve performance, because "more contracting could produce economies in some (often more peripheral) activities, freeing up part of a school system's discretionary budget for use on the core educational function." Other studies suggest that the existence of out-sourcing itself does not necessarily lead to better outcomes. Meier and O'Toole (2001) find that networks rather than contracts are associated with higher service performance. O'Toole and Meier (2004) use the Texas Assessment of Academic Skills (TAAS) as a performance indicator to evaluate the effects of contracting out. Controlling for race/ethnicity of students, poverty, tax wealth per student, revenue per student, and state aid percentage, they conclude that contracting is not positively related to school district performance, but suggest that systematic study of contracting effects on service quality is worthy of further exploration (O'Toole and Meier, 2004, p. 344).

Public, for-profit, and nonprofit organizations offer distinctive advantages that can enhance the effectiveness, efficiency, and equity outcomes of out-sourcing (Andrews and Entwistle, 2010). Nonprofits in particular are viewed as more favorable vendors when outsourcing for health and human services because "nonprofit organizations are thought to share similar missions with government" and a nonprofit "might draw on its own private philanthropic resources to augment services it delivers under government contract" (Brown et al., 2006). Similarly, LeRoux (2009, p. 166) argues that nonprofits are more likely to hold public values transmitted by government funding, and "these values favor democratic participation, responsive service delivery, and equitable distribution of resources."

## Collaboration and Effectiveness

Collaborative management is a concept that "emphasizes engaging partici-pants across the boundaries of organizations or sectors to solve problems in a formal, consensus-oriented, and deliberative relationships" . The fundamen-tal reason for the increasing collaboration between the public sector and the private sector may be the realization that many public issues are too complex for a single entity to adequately address . Therefore, the public sector, through efforts to increase purposive collaboration, may gain more resources—facilities, information, expertise, professionals, and specialists—that will improve the effectiveness of public service delivery.

In the arena of public health, many issues represent complex and wicked problems because they are constructed with a set of conflicts: inadequate provision, rising needs, social and economic influences, different values, a lot of interest groups, and inequalities. As Brunton and Galloway (2016, p. 163) have suggested, "Public health systems present the epitome of problem 'wickedness': no matter how many resources are dedicated to their resolution, there are never enough."

Empirical studies have exhibited mixed results regarding how contracting could influence health outcomes. Sinclair and Whitford (2015, p. 1638) assert that "collaboration theory suggests that greater participation of the LHD in the system (greater centrality) and greater participation of a variety of organizations and agencies could lead to higher levels of effectiveness in accomplishing core local health functions." Rohrer (2004) explains that the state of Wisconsin funds LHDs for agreed-upon outcomes of contracting, and emphasizes that contracting for outcomes could be an effective mechanism, although health outcomes are difficult to specify. Agbodzakey (2012) compares collaborative governance of HIV health services in two South Florida counties and finds that collaboration among stakeholders enhances efforts in effectively managing and/or addressing complex relevant problems. However, demonstrates that the state of California contracting with health maintenance organizations was associated with a substantial increase in government spending, but no corresponding improvement in infant health outcomes.

Existing studies typically suggest that collaboration (such as outsourcing) is a positive factor to be pursued by managers because it contributes to solving public problems by producing more effective, efficient, and flexible policies, and improved outcomes or effectiveness . Yet, Dickinson and Glasby (2010) point out that in many cases collaborative approaches are adopted because of internal and external pressures based on the assumption that collaboration will be effective, rather than the belief that they are effective (Silvia 2018). As a result, many governments invest substantial time and money in collaboration without knowing whether what they are doing is effectively tackling the problem (Koontz and Thomas, 2006). Below, we present a theoretical framework for understanding how the characteristics of services may influence the success of contracting out, when success is defined by improved service quality, or in this case, community health outcomes.

**Transaction Costs and Outsourcing Outcomes: A Theoretical Framework**

The concept of transaction cost was initially introduced by Coase (1937) in "The nature of the firm," which identifies the less visible costs of transactions that exist in addition to the production costs made visible through the price mechanism. Elaborating on Coase, Williamson (1981) proposed two behavioral assumptions from human nature for understanding the transaction cost approach: bounded rationality and opportunism. With bounded rationality, it is impossible to deal with complexity in all contractually relevant respects, since agents/human actors experience limits in solving complex problems; thus incomplete contracting is the best that can be achieved . As circumstances change, opportunism may occur to seek self-interest, which is a primary hazard threatening the reliable conduct of transactions . Transaction costs can be understood through three critical dimensions: uncertainty, recurrence, and asset specificity . Williamson argues that when the degree of unpredictability in transaction outcomes (uncertainty) is high, the frequency with which transactions recur is high, and the fixed investment that is specialized to a particular transaction (asset specificity) is large, then transaction costs will rise accordingly.

### Asset specificity

Asset specificity refers to whether investments are specialized to a particular transaction (Williamson 1981). Put it another way, "asset specificity has reference to the degree to which an asset can be redeployed to alternative uses and by alternative users without sacrifice of productive value" (Williamson, 1991, p. 282). In the transaction cost approach, much of the explanatory power turns on asset specificity, which gives rise to bilateral dependency, brings possible disturbances, and poses added contracting hazards (Williamson, 1991, 2008). Asset specificity can become an issue at the outset between the buyer and initial winning bidder, during contract implementation, and at the contract renewal interval. Asset specificity can arise in any of three ways: site specificity, physical asset specificity, and human asset specificity (Williamson, 1981). Assets that are unspecialized among users, or low asset specificity, pose few hazards, since buyers in these circumstances can easily turn to alternative sources and suppliers can sell output intended for one buyer to other buyers without difficulty (Williamson, 1981). With large specific capital or high asset specificity, nevertheless, the supplier is effectively "locked into" the transaction to a significant degree. As a consequence, the buyer cannot turn to alternative sources of supply and obtain the item on favorable terms, since the cost of supply from unspecialized capital is presumably great. The buyer is thus committed to the transaction as well (Williamson, 1981).

### Service measurability

Alchian and Demsetz (1972) describe "metering the output" in economic organizations which can facilitate the payment of rewards in accordance with productivity. Measuring the output matters, because productivity will be greater with rewards and productivity closely correlated. On the contrary, productivity will be smaller if the organization meters poorly with rewards and productivity (pp. 778–779). Williamson (1981) also emphasizes metering the output in transactions, arguing that "the internal organizational counterpart for uncertainty is the ease with which the productivity of human assets can be evaluated" (p. 564).

Brown and Potoski (2003) extend the concept of metering the output of human assets to general service measurability which refers to "how difficult it is for the contracting organization to measure the outcomes of the service, to monitor the activities required to deliver the service, or both of these" (p. 444). Ease of measurement or service measurability refers to how easily and straightforwardly public managers can assess the quantity or quality of services . Easy service measurability can help the contracting organization identify and assess performance, reduce disturbance and uncertainty, and thus lower transaction costs. Service measurability or ease of measurement has been identified as an important component of strategic decision-making defining the risks of privatization .

## Hypothesized Relationships: Contracting for Services with High and Low Transaction Costs

Vining and Globerman (1999) and Brown and Potoski (2005) present a systematic framework based on asset specificity and service measurability to classify transaction costs, and this has been used to predict which services governments are most likely to contract out. We extend the use of this theoretical framework to examine the effects of outsourcing lower versus higher transaction cost services. We first describe the types of health services with lower and higher transaction costs, then employ this framework in our analysis.

### Higher transaction cost services
Public health services with higher transaction costs are those with higher levels of asset specificity and higher service meterability (that is, more difficult to measure). point out that health care-related activities generally have high asset specificity and difficult service measurability. Brown and Potoski (2005) conducted a survey in which 36 city managers and mayors across the country rated 64 public services. The results show that public health programs have high transaction costs as a whole. For example, they find that drug and alcohol treatment, as well as operation of mental health programs and facilities, have very high transaction costs. Brown and Potoski (2005) maintain that high transaction cost services pose the highest risk of contract failure because: (1) high asset specificity may attract fewer bidders and reduce competition; and (2) it is difficult for public health agencies to monitor outcomes. Yet, Brown and Potoski (2005) also suggest that the risks of outsourcing failure could be

offset if: (1) public managers are vigilant in monitoring vendor performance; (2) public managers find more bidders; (3) public managers choose nonprofits as vendors, as they hold inherently altruistic motives; and (4) vendors have specialized expertise in tackling tough cases. Accordingly, we argue that outsourcing high transaction cost services may have consequences of producing lower service quality, measured here by poorer community health outcomes. Nevertheless, a more robust market (increased competition) and choosing nonprofits as vendors may help offset the high risks of contract failure.

**Lower transaction cost services**

Public health services with lower transaction costs are those with lower levels of asset specificity and lower service meterability (easier to measure). Outsourcing services with low transaction costs are more likely to lead to "high potential for efficiency and cost savings and low risk of contract failure," because public managers can easily specify the outcomes and replace current vendors with alternatives on the vibrant market once their performance is unsatisfied (Brown and Potoski, 2005, p. 332). One example of low transaction cost service is sanitary inspection. Quality of sanitary inspection is easy to gauge, because it is quite easy to observe hygienic conditions. We expect that contracting out health services with low transaction costs (low asset specificity and easy service measurability) will be linked to greater community health outcomes. Table 3.1 presents some examples of public health services that fall into each of these categories of transaction costs.

## DATA AND METHODOLOGICAL APPROACH

The data used in this study come from multiple sources. In order to capture the activities of contracting out by LHDs, this study employs data from the 2016 National Profile of Local Health Department Study that was conducted by the National Association of County and City Health Officials (NACCHO). The 2016 survey had a response rate of 76 percent (National Association of County and City Health Officials, 2017a). After data-cleaning, our analysis includes 1662 local health departments.

In order to construct valid measures of transaction costs, we followed Brown and Potoski's (2003) measurement approach, by asking a small group of public health experts to rating transaction costs (asset specificity and service measurability) for 44 local health services using their professional judgment. We provided them with definitions of asset specificity and service measurability, and asked them to rate each the degree of asset specificity and service measurability on a scale of 1 (lowest) to 5 (highest) for each of the 44 services. Table 3.1 shows the average ratings of asset specificity and service measurability for each of these services.

*Table 3.1*     *Average asset specificity and service measurability ratings*

| Service | Asset specificity | Service measurability |
|---|---|---|
| *1. Immunization Services* | | |
| Adult immunization | 3.17 | 2.17 |
| Childhood immunization | 3.33 | 2.17 |
| *2. Screening for Diseases/Conditions* | | |
| HIV/AIDS | 3.50 | 2.83 |
| Other STDs | 3.33 | 2.83 |
| Tuberculosis | 3.33 | 2.33 |
| Cancer | 4.00 | 3.00 |
| Cardiovascular disease | 3.33 | 2.50 |
| Diabetes | 2.83 | 2.33 |
| High blood pressure | 2.50 | 2.00 |
| Blood lead | 3.50 | 2.83 |
| BMI (Body Mass Index) | 2.00 | 1.67 |
| *3. Treatment for Communicable Diseases Services* | | |
| HIV/AIDS | 4.50 | 3.17 |
| Other STDs | 4.00 | 2.83 |
| Tuberculosis | 4.33 | 3.17 |
| *4. Maternal and Child Health Services* | | |
| Family planning | 3.33 | 2.67 |
| Prenatal care | 3.67 | 3.00 |
| Obstetrical care | 3.83 | 3.00 |
| WIC (Women, Infants & Children) | 3.17 | 2.67 |
| MCH (Maternal and Child Health) home visits | 3.50 | 2.83 |
| EPSDT (Early and Periodic Screening, Diagnostic and Treatment) | 3.50 | 3.17 |
| Well child clinic | 3.17 | 3.00 |
| *5. Other Health Services* | | |
| Comprehensive primary care | 4.00 | 3.17 |
| Home health care | 4.17 | 3.50 |
| Oral health | 4.17 | 3.33 |
| Behavior/mental health services | 4.50 | 3.67 |
| Substance abuse services | 4.67 | 3.50 |
| *6. Epidemiology and Surveillance Activities* | | |
| Communicable/infectious disease | 4.17 | 3.33 |
| Chronic disease | 3.50 | 3.50 |

| Service | Asset specificity | Service measurability |
|---|---|---|
| Injury | 3.33 | 3.00 |
| Behavior risk factors | 3.33 | 3.33 |
| Environmental health | 4.00 | 3.00 |
| Syndromic surveillance | 3.67 | 3.33 |
| Maternal and child health | 3.67 | 3.17 |
| *7. Population-Based Primary Prevention Activities* | | |
| Injury | 2.83 | 3.50 |
| Violence | 3.33 | 4.00 |
| Unintended pregnancy | 3.17 | 3.83 |
| Chronic disease | 3.33 | 3.67 |
| Nutrition | 3.33 | 4.00 |
| Physical activity | 3.17 | 3.50 |
| Tobacco | 3.00 | 3.17 |
| Substance abuse | 3.83 | 4.00 |
| Mental illness | 4.17 | 4.33 |
| *8. Regulation, Inspection and/or Licensing Activities* | | |
| Tobacco retailers | 3.17 | 2.83 |
| Smoke-free ordinances | 3.00 | 3.00 |

*Note:* These asset specificity and service measureability rankings represent averaged scores from a group of public health experts who were asked to rank these two types of transaction costs on a scale of 1 (lowest) to 5 (highest).

Based on these values we selected four services, one that exemplifies each quadrant of the four-cell matrix presented in Table 3.2, arraying services along the dimensions of high and low for the two types of transaction costs: asset specificity and service measurability.

Since we are interested in knowing whether contracting out for these services is linked to corresponding health outcomes, we conduct a set of multivariate regression analyses in which the extent of contracting for these four specific services function as our key independent variables of interest: mental health prevention services (high asset specificity and difficult service measurability), HIV/AIDS/STDs treatment services (high asset specificity and easy service measurability), pregnancy prevention services (low asset specificity and difficulty service measurability), and tobacco regulation services (low asset specificity and easy service measurability). We control for several other factors in our models, including community demographics and market conditions (degree of competition) within the LHD's service range. The data for the demographic measures were obtained from the 2018 County Health Rankings and Roadmaps and the 2011–2015 American Community Survey 5-Year Estimates by the US Census.

*Table 3.2    Examples of public health services with lower and higher transaction costs*

| | Public health services with high asset specificity | Public health services with low asset specificity |
|---|---|---|
| Public health services with difficult (higher) service measurability | Mental illness prevention (asset specificity = 4.17; service measurability = 4.33) | Pregnancy prevention (asset specificity = 3.17; service measurability = 3.83) |
| Public health services with easier (lower) service measurability | HIV/AIDS/Other STDs Treatment (asset specificity = 4.25; service measurability = 3.00) | Tobacco prevention (asset specificity = 3.00; service measurability = 3.17) |

*Note:* These asset specificity and service measurability values represent averaged scores from a group of public health experts who were asked to rank these services in terms of their transaction costs on a scale of 1 (lowest) to 5 (highest). The services that appear in these four quadrants are a subset of the services reported in Table 3.1.

**Dependent Variables**

To measure health outcomes related to these four services, we rely on data from the County Health Rankings and Roadmaps (CHRR). The County Health Rankings were created by the Robert Wood Johnson Foundation and the University of Wisconsin Population Health Institute. The data are standardized to "measure the health of nearly all counties (and county equivalents) in the nation and rank them within states" (County Health Rankings and Roadmaps, 2018). The rankings are based on a model of population health that includes health outcomes (length and quality of life) as well as health factors (health behaviors, clinical care, social and economic factors, and physical environment). We examine health outcomes at the level of the county in this study, based on available data from CHRR and contracting data of local health departments from the NACCHO.[1]

In constructing our outcome variables, we identified four distinct public health services with transaction costs ranging from low to high levels in Table 3.2 as the dependent variables in this research: frequent mental distress (outcome relating to outsourcing mental health prevention services), sexually transmitted infections (outcome relating to outsourcing HIV/AIDS/STDs treatment services), teen births (outcome relating to outsourcing unintended pregnancy prevention services), and adult smoking rate (outcome relating to outsourcing tobacco regulation services). More specifically, "frequent mental distress" is the percentage of adults who reported more than 14 days in response to the question, "Now, thinking about your mental health, which includes stress, depression, and problems with emotions, for how many days during the past 30 days was your mental health not good?" "Sexually transmitted infections" (STIs) refer to the number of newly diagnosed chlamydia cases per 100 000 population of a county in a given time period (CHRR, 2019). "Teen births" is the number of births to female ages 15–19 per 1000 females in a county in a given time period (CHRR, 2019). "Adult smoking" measures the percentage of the adult population in a county who both report that they currently smoke every day or most days, and have smoked at least 100 cigarettes in their lifetime (CHRR, 2019).

**Independent Variables**

The purpose of our study is to assess whether contracting out for various health services is linked to greater health outcomes at the community level. "Contracting out" is defined as to "pay another organization to perform this activity or service on behalf of your LHD" (National Association of County and City Health Officials, 2017a). We measure contracting out as "%Buy/ (Make+Buy)" by calculating the percentage of services funded by LHD that are contracted out.

While the extent of contracting for each of these four categories of services are the primary variables of interest, we control for a series of demographic factors that are likely to shape community health outcomes, including the percentage of the county population with some college, percentage unemployed, percentage aged 65 and over, percentage non-Hispanic white, as well as log of population. All the models are estimated using ordinary least squares regression with robust standard errors. We present descriptive statistics for all variables in Table 3.3.

*Table 3.3    Descriptive statistics*

| Variables | Obs | Mean | Std. Dev. | Min | Max |
|---|---|---|---|---|---|
| *Outcome variables* | | | | | |
| 1. Frequent mental distress (%) | 1662 | 12.248 | 1.874 | 8.035 | 19.176 |
| 2. Sexually transmitted infections (per 100 000 population) | 1623 | 359.871 | 207.077 | 55 | 1422.2 |
| 3. Teen births | 1626 | 32.113 | 14.439 | 2.822 | 128.651 |
| 4. Adult smoking (%) | 1662 | 17.871 | 3.483 | 6.735 | 31.737 |
| *Predictor variables* | | | | | |
| 1. Mental illness prevention (%) (asset specificity = 4.17; service measurability = 4.33) | 336 | 18.006 | 34.922 | 0 | 100 |
| 2. Treatment for HIV/AIDS/Other STDs (%) (asset specificity = 4.25; service measurability = 3) | 1268 | 10.016 | 25.311 | 0 | 100 |
| 3. Pregnancy prevention (%) (asset specificity = 3.17; service measurability = 3.83) | 911 | 4.007 | 16.833 | 0 | 100 |
| 4. Tobacco prevention (%) (asset specificity = 3.00; service measurability = 3.17) | 1314 | 6.012 | 19.853 | 0 | 100 |
| *Control Variables* | | | | | |
| 1. Some college (%) | 1662 | 58.665 | 10.970 | 19.250 | 85.772 |
| 2. Unemployment (%) | 1662 | 5.133 | 1.760 | 1.746 | 35.715 |
| 3. People over 65 (%) | 1662 | 18.271 | 4.296 | 5.101 | 38.841 |
| 4. Non-Hispanic White (%) | 1662 | 79.069 | 17.789 | 3.552 | 97.843 |
| 5. Log(population) | 1662 | 4.638 | 0.636 | 2.840 | 7.006 |

## STUDY RESULTS AND NEW INSIGHTS

The extent to which LHDs buy, or contract out for, health services varies across counties. On average, LHDs contract out 18.01 percent of mental illness prevention services, 10.02 percent of HIV/AIDS/STDs treatment services, 4.01 percent of pregnancy prevention services, and 6.01 percent of tobacco retailer regulation and smoke-free ordinances regulation services. Table 3.4 displays the ordinary least squares (OLS) results which reveal the relationship between outsourcing for these services and their corresponding community health outcomes.

In model 1, the outcome variable is the percentage of adult population experiencing frequent mental distress and the predictor variable is public sector contracting for mental illness prevention, a service with high transaction costs. Theory suggests that contracting out high transaction cost public health may lead to diminished service quality (worse health outcomes). We find no relationship between outsourcing mental illness prevention and rates of frequent mental distress, suggesting that contracting for this service is not statistically linked to either better or worse health outcomes. Given that mental illness prevention is categorized as a high transaction cost service, one implication of this finding is that public managers should not expect to see improved outcomes from contracting high transaction cost services are involved. The results for model 1 in Table 3.4 also reveal that communities have lower rates of adults experiencing frequent mental distress when the population is more highly educated, employed, and the population is smaller.

Moving to model 2 in Table 3.4, we estimate the impact of contracting out for HIV/AIDS/STDs treatment on a corresponding health outcome measured as sexually transmitted infections per 100 000 population. The findings demonstrate that contracting out for services with mixed transaction costs such as treatment for HIV/AIDS/STDs (high asset specificity and lower service measurability) is linked to improved health outcomes (lower STIs per 100 000). Again, we find community demographics also shape lower STI rates, such as size of the aged population. Turning to model 3, we find a negative relationship between outsourcing pregnancy prevention services and teen births; in other words, as contracting for pregnancy prevention services increases, communities tend to experience lower rates of teen births (improved health outcomes). Pregnancy prevention is a service with mixed transaction cost characteristics (low asset specificity and higher/difficult service measurability). The results also reveal that jurisdictions have lower teen births when the county demographics include higher education and employment rates, and larger elderly and white populations.

Lastly, model 4 estimates the impact of LHDs contracting out for tobacco prevention services on adult smoking rates in the county. According to the scores generated by our public health experts, tobacco prevention is a lower transaction cost service, and thus this finding that service contracting is linked to improved health outcomes (adult smoking rates) is consistent with our theory-informed prediction. The results in Table 3.4 also indicate that jurisdictions have lower rates of adult smokers when the population has higher percentages of education, employment, older residents, and racial minorities.

*Table 3.4*　Relationship between contracting out for public health services and health outcomes for those services

| | Model 1 Frequent mental distress (%) | Model 2 Sexually transmitted infections (per 100 000 population) | Model 3 Teen births (numbers) | Model 4 Adult smoking (%) |
|---|---|---|---|---|
| Contracting: Mental illness prevention (high asset specificity, difficult service measurability) | -0.042 (0.002) | | | |
| Contracting: Treatment for HIV/AIDS/STDs prevention (high asset specificity, easier service measurability) | | -0.060** (0.172) | | |
| Contracting: pregnancy prevention (low asset specificity, easier service measurability) | | | -0.066** (0.018) | |
| Contracting: tobacco prevention (low asset specificity, easier service measurability) | | | | -0.071*** (0.003) |
| Some College | -0.620***(0.009) | 0.036 (0.592) | -0.540*** (0.050) | -0.613*** (0.012) |
| Unemployed | 0.223**(0.074) | 0.011 (5.570) | 0.258*** (0.529) | 0.163** (0.115) |
| People over 65 | 0.020(0.020) | -0.159*** (1.070) | -0.158*** (0.093) | -0.221*** (0.023) |
| Non-Hispanic White | -0.040(0.006) | -0.642** (0.398) | -0.136*** (0.028) | 0.188*** (0.006) |
| Log (Population) | 0.143*(0.062) | -0.028 (4.456) | -0.147* (0.338) | -0.058 (0.0789) |
| Cons | (1.236) | (84.180) | (6.397) | (1.460) |
| N | 336 | 1254 | 904 | 1314 |
| R² | 0.542 | 0.508 | 0.554 | 0.472 |

*Notes:* * $p < 0.05$; ** $p < 0.01$; *** $p < 0.001$. Robust standard errors are reported in parentheses. Results are shown in standardized beta.

# IMPLICATIONS AND LESSONS LEARNED

The results of this study lend support to the notion that outsourcing can generate public value by improving community-level outcomes, but there are some important caveats that must be heeded. We find that contracting out health services with lower asset specificity and easier service measurability, or lower transaction costs, are more likely to be linked to improved conditions in the form of better service outcomes. Similarly, services with mixed transaction costs (those that rank high on either asset specificity or service measurability, but lower on the other dimension) can also be linked to improved service outcomes, although contract managers may need to invest more time in monitoring and oversight of contracted services under conditions of mixed transaction costs.

Theory suggests that contracting should be avoided for services that are characterized by high transaction costs. Our results show that when contracting for these types of services there are no discernable adverse effects, but neither are there any gains in service effectiveness. We also know that public organizations often do in fact contract for high transaction cost services such as mental health prevention, because the conditions these services address are highly complex and require specialized capacities or expertise that the public organization lacks. We also know that public organizations often struggle to clearly define the scope of work in contracting out these complex services, as well as struggle to specify what successful performance should look like (LeRoux, 2007). Given these realities, nonprofits may be preferrable to for-profits as contracting partners for complex or high transaction cost services, as they lack the profit-maximizing incentives that lead to opportunism. Moreover, they have the legal authority to engage in fundraising, and solicitation of corporate and foundation funds, allowing them to bring their own resources to bear on community health problems. In this sense, contracting with nonprofits may generate additional public value.

Relatedly, previous work has shown that nonprofits act as "trusted messengers" (LeRoux and Krawcyzk, 2014) among those they serve, and clients of marginalized groups in particular may be more receptive to messaging that comes from a known, trusted community organization messages than from a government agency. In this same way, nonprofit health providers might be more effective in imparting health advice and instructions than a public health department. In the case of pregnancy prevention services, for example, Planned Parenthood is a nonprofit that may serve as an LHD contractor in many places, and as a well-known brand for providing safe and compassionate care for low-income and uninsured women, it may be more effective at reducing teen birth rates than the county health department. While we lack evidence to make causal claims about this, it is logically plausible and presents a question for future research and theory testing.

This study offers evidence-based guidance for local health department directors as well as public procurement managers when they are facing "make or buy" decisions: (1) public agencies can maintain their autonomy and power through contracting activities; (2) contracting out lower transaction cost services is more often linked to better health outcomes or higher quality; (3) public agency contract managers should make outsourcing decisions based on an analysis of transaction costs, and be prepared to scale monitoring mechanisms and oversight protocols to the level of transaction costs associated with the service(s) being contracted; and (4) nonprofits may be preferable to for-profits as contracting partners for complex or high transaction cost services.

In the US, government is only one actor in the complex health services establishment. In recent years, public demands for health services have become greater, given that the aged population has reached its highest level in human history; public health emergencies such as the coronavirus pandemic have occurred unexpectedly, requiring flexibility and swift action; and health care is far more expensive in the US than any other industrialized country. Correspondingly, contracting out public health services represents a form of innovation in health service delivery which is based on "a recognition that arrangements for the provision of goods and services may be separated from arrangements for their production" . Through contracting, governments and public health service vendors may tap into the flexibility, innovation, and capacity of the private sector while retaining provision rights and oversight of production. Such an arrangement allows local public health departments to fulfill the expanding needs for public goods and services and create public value.

Public health contractors contribute their specialized skills, professional expertise, fundraising capacity, and other assets to collaborative service delivery in order to improve effectiveness and outcomes. For their part, public health departments engaging in outsourcing could enhance public value creation by building opportunities for civic learning into the provider selection process, and require contractors to do the same in the service delivery process. For example, LHDs engaging in outsourcing can introduce contractors on their websites, require contractors to inform service recipients of complaint mechanisms or due process reporting, and conduct surveys to investigate how citizens evaluate the services that they receive from publicly funded private providers. Such efforts to ensure transparency and responsiveness under conditions of outsourcing may help reduce information asymmetry and general distrust towards contracting out for services.

There are a number of limitations of this study that must be noted. Our analysis relies on data from one point in time, and is thus subject to the caveats that come with cross-sectional studies. Data limitations also prevent us from stating with certainty the contract partners that local health departments select for outsourcing specific services. Qualitative research obtained through interviews would further our understanding about how LHDs' directors think about contracting decisions, and to what extent they perceive outsourcing to increase service quality or enhance community health outcomes. Despite these limitations, this analysis moves us one step further in our understanding of contracting consequences, particularly as they relate to service quality and effectiveness.

## NOTE

1.  To set up a final dataset for examining the correlation between LHD contract-ing activities and health outcomes, we combine the above datasets by Federal Information Processing Standard (FIPS) county code that is included in mul-tiple datasets. However, not all LHDs are county-level government agencies. Approximately 69 percent of LHDs are county-based, 8 percent of LHDs serve multiple counties, and 20 percent of LHDs serve cities or towns (in New England) (National Association of County and City Health Officials, 2017b). We turn some county-level health outcomes into multi-county average values by using the 2018 CHRR data in order to match with those LHDs that serve multiple counties in the 2016 NACCHO data. As a result, only county and multi-county LHDs, and corresponding county health outcomes, exist in the final dataset for analysis.

## REFERENCES

Agbodzakey, J.K. (2012). Collaborative governance of HIV health services planning councils in Broward and Palm Beach counties of South Florida. *Public Organization Review* 12 (2): 107–126.

Agranoff, R., and McGuire, M. (2004). *Collaborative Public Management: New Strategies for Local Governments*. Washington, DC: Georgetown University Press.

Alchian, A.A., and Demsetz, H. (1972). Production, information costs, and economic organization. *American Economic Review* 62 (5): 777–795.

American Public Health Association (APHA) (2019). What is public health? https://www.apha.org/what-is-public-health.

Amirkhanyan, A. (2008). Collaborative performance measurement: Examining and explaining the prevalence of collaboration in state and local government contracts. *Journal of Public Administration Research and Theory* 19 (3): 523–554.

Andrews, R., and Entwistle, T. (2010). Does cross-sectoral partnership deliver? An empirical exploration of public service effectiveness, efficiency, and equity. *Journal of Public Administration Research and Theory* 20 (3): 679–701.

Ansell, C., and Gash, A. (2008).Collaborative governance in theory and practice. *Journal of Public Administration Research and Theory* 18 (4): 543–571.

Boyne, G.A. (1998a.) Bureaucratic theory meets reality: Public choice and service contracting in US local government. *Public Administration Review* 58 (6): 474–484.

Boyne, G.A. (1998b). *Public Choice Theory and Local Government*. London: Macmillan Press.

Brown, T.L., and Potoski, M. (2003). Transaction costs and institutional explanations for government service production decisions. *Journal of Public Administration Research and Theory* 13 (4): 441–468.

Brown, T.L., and Potoski, M. (2005). Transaction costs and contracting: The practitioner perspective. *Public Performance and Management Review* 28 (3): 326–351.

Brown, T.L., Potoski, M., and Van Slyke, D.M. (2006). Managing public service contracts: Aligning values, institutions, and markets. *Public Administration Review* 66 (3): 323–331. https://doi.org/10.1111/j.1540-6210.2006.00590.x.

Brudney, J.L., Fernandez, S., Ryu, J.E., and Wright, D.S. (2005). Exploring and explaining contracting out: Patterns among the American states. *Journal of Public Administration Research and Theory* 15 (3): 393–419. https://doi.org/10.1093/jopart/mui019.

Brunton, M.A., and Galloway, C. (2016). The role of "organic public relations" in communicating wicked public health issues. *Journal of Communication Management* 20 (2): 162–177

Buchanan, J.M., and Tullock, G. (1962). *The Calculus of Consent*, Vol. 3. Ann Arbor, MI: University of Michigan Press.

Coase, R.H. (1937). The nature of the firm. *Economica* 4 (16): 386–405.

County Health Rankings and Roadmaps (CHRR) (2019). Accessed July 1, 2019 at https://www.countyhealthrankings.org/.

Dickinson, H., and Glasby, J. (2010). Why partnership working doesn't work: Pitfalls, problems and possibilities in English health and social care. *Public Management Review* 12 (6): 811–828. https://doi.org/10.1080/14719037.2010.488861.

Duggan, M. (2004). Does contracting out increase the efficiency of government programs? Evidence from Medicaid HMOs. *Journal of Public Economics* 88 (12): 2549–2572. https://doi.org/10.1016/j.jpubeco.2003.08.003.

Ferris, J. (1986). The decision to contract out: An empirical analysis. *Urban Affairs Review* 22 (2): 289–311. https://doi.org/10.1177/004208168602200206.

Hodge, G.A. (2000). *Privatization: An International Review of Performance.* Theoretical Lenses on Public Policy series. Boulder, CO: Westview Press.

Issel, L.M., Olorunsaiye, C., Snebold, L., and Handler, A. (2015). Relationships among providing maternal, child, and adolescent health services; implementing various financial strategy responses; and performance of local health departments. *American Journal of Public Health* 105 (S2): S244–S251.

Keane, C., Marx, J., and Ricci, E. (2002). Services privatized in local health departments: A national survey of practices and perspectives. *American Journal of Public Health* 92 (8): 1250–1254.

Koontz, T.M., and Thomas, C.W. (2006). What do we know and need to know about the environmental outcomes of collaborative management. *Public Administration Review* 66 (s1): 111–121.

LeRoux, K. (2007). *Service Contracting: A Local Government Guide.* Washington, DC: ICMA Press

LeRoux, K. (2009). Managing stakeholder demands: Balancing responsiveness to clients and funding agents in nonprofit social service organizations. *Administration and Society* 41 (2): 158–184.

LeRoux, K., and Krawczyk, K. (2014). Can nonprofit organizations increase voter turnout? Findings from an agency-based voter mobilization experiment. *Nonprofit and Voluntary Sector Quarterly* 43 (2): 272–292.

McGuire, M. (2006). Collaborative public management: Assessing what we know and how we know it. *Public Administration Review* 66 (s1): 33–43.

Meier, K.J., and O'Toole, L.J. (2001). Managerial strategies and behavior in networks: A model with evidence from US public education. *Journal of Public Administration Research and Theory* 11 (3): 271–294.

National Association of County and City Health Officials (NACCHO) (2017a). 2016 National Profile of Local Health Departments. National Association of County and City Health Officials.

National Association of County and City Health Officials (NACCHO) (2017b). 2017 Profile Report. National Association of County and City Health Officials. Accessed May 10, 2019 at http://nacchoprofilestudy.org/wp-content/uploads/2017/10/ProfileReport_Aug2017_final.pdf.

O'Toole, L.J., and Meier, K.J. (2004). Parkinson's Law and the New Public Managment? Contracting determinants and service quality consequences in public education. *Public Administration Review* 64 (3): 297–307.

O'Leary, R., and Vij, N. (2012). Collaborative public management: Where have we been and where are we going? *American Review of Public Administration* 42 (5): 507–522. https://doi.org/10.1177/0275074012445780.

Oakerson, R.J., and Parks, R.B. (1989). Local government constitutions: A different view of metropolitan governance. *American Review of Public Administration* 19 (4): 279–294.

Oakerson, R.J., and Parks, R.B. (2011). The study of local public economies: Multi-organizational, multi-level institutional analysis and development. *Policy Studies Journal* 39 (1): 147–167.

Parks, R.B., and Oakerson, R.J. (2000). Regionalism, localism, and metropolitan governance: Suggestions from the research program on local public economies. *State and Local Government Review* 32 (3): 169–179.

Ran, B., and Qi, H. (2018). Contingencies of power sharing in collaborative governance. *American Review of Public Administration* 48 (8): 836–851.

Reich, M.R. (2002). *Public–Private Partnerships for Public Health*. Cambridge, MA: Harvard University Press.

Rohrer, J. (2004). Performance contracting for public health: The potential and the implications. *Journal of Public Health Management and Practice* 10 (1): 23–25.

Romzek, B.S., and Johnston, J. (2002). Effective contract implementation and management: A preliminary model. *Journal of Public Administration Research and Theory* 12 (3): 423–453.

Romzek, B.S., and Johnston, J. (2005). State social services contracting: Exploring the determinants of effective contract accountability. *Public Administration Review* 65 (4): 436–449.

Savas, E.S. (2000). *Privatization and Public–Private Partnerships* (2nd edn). New York: Seven Bridges Press.

Silvia, C. (2018). Evaluating collaboration: The solution to one problem often causes another. *Public Administration Review* 78 (3): 472–478. https://doi.org/10.1111/puar.12888.

Simon, H.A. (1957). *Models of Man, Social and National*. New York: Wiley.

Sinclair, A., and Whitford, A. (2015). Effects of participation and collaboration on perceived effectiveness of core public health functions. *American Journal of Public Health* 105 (8): 1638–1645.

Vining, A.R., and Globerman, S. (1999). Contracting-out health care services: a conceptual framework. *Health Policy* 46 (2): 77–96. https://doi.org/10.1016/S0168-8510(98)00056-6.

Williamson, O. (1981). The economics of organization: The transaction cost approach. *American Journal of Sociology* 87 (1): 548–577.

Williamson, O.E. (1991). Comparative economic organization: The analysis of discrete structural alternatives. *Administrative Science Quarterly* 36 (2): 269–296.

Williamson, O. (1999). Public and private bureaucracies: A transaction cost economics perspectives. *Journal of Law, Economics, and Organization* 15 (1): 306–342.

Williamson, O. (2008). Outsourcing: Transaction cost economics and supply chain management. *Journal of Supply Chain Management* 44 (2): 5–16. https://doi.org/10.1111/j.1745-493X.2008.00051.x.

# 4. The role of community action agencies in facilitating successful sustainable development in American cities

## Nathaniel S. Wright and Tony G. Reames

Over the past several decades in the United States (US), community-based nongovernmental organizations and nonprofit community action agencies (CAAs) have emerged as leaders in the hollow state, with a growing capacity for undertaking community sustainability projects (Agyeman, 2005; Portney and Berry, 2014; Portney and Cuttler, 2010). The dependence on CAAs to meet community sustainability goals reflects a profound shift away from large bureaucratic government agencies and toward more flexible, less rule-bound organizations (Osborne and Gaebler, 1993; Smith and Lipsky, 2009). CAAs represent an alternative market strategy to assist local municipalities with the provision of public goods and meeting community needs. Despite sporadic and often inadequate financial support, CAAs have assumed responsibility for many aspects of sustainable development, including residential weatherization, energy conservation, transportation, and the provision of housing and shelter to urban and rural communities (Agyeman and Evans, 2003; Marwell, 2009; Rubin, 2000). Some of these communities are and have been primarily homes for inner city African Americans, migrant farmworkers, and undocumented immigrants. A characteristic shared by all these communities has been the lack of government action and investment from outsiders to preserve or build sustainable communities.

To some extent, CAAs have been successful in their pursuit of community sustainability (Agyeman, 2005; Portney and Berry, 2010, 2016). Case studies have been conducted to document the role of community-based nonprofits in pursuing sustainability initiatives in localities (Portney and Cuttler, 2010). Evaluative research seems to suggest that community-based nonprofits can promote sustainability efforts in cities and towns, sometimes more effectively than statewide or national groups (Stokes et al., 2014; Lyth et al., 2017). Yet beyond case and evaluative studies, there is little empirical evidence examining the relationship between various organizational and managerial capacities on community sustainability outcomes. Many have examined and expressed the importance of organizational, socioeconomic, demographic characteristics in influencing local sustainability efforts by local government (Krause, 2011; Saha and Paterson, 2008; Wang et al., 2012); however, few explicitly explore these linkages in the context of CAAs or other nongovernmental organizations.

Despite these limitations, policymakers at the municipal level of government are taking extraordinary steps to work with the nonprofit sector to alter the manner in which decisions are made concerning sustainability practices (Portney and Cuttler, 2010). These same policymakers are also altering the manner in which decisions are made with respect to how economic development affects their capacity to manage sustainability efforts (Wang et al., 2012). There are a multitude of reasons why these shifts in decision-making are occurring, but a primary reason for doing so is a heightened awareness among policymakers about the importance of having the support of nonprofit and grassroots organizations in the adoption of sustainability and smart growth policies (Portney and Cuttler, 2010).

Understanding which factors promote community sustainability efforts by CAAs is important for several reasons. First, the number of CAAs operating in the US has grown exponentially, and thus their presence in community sustainability is likely to increase in the future (Galaskiewicz et al., 2016). Second, these organizations are increasingly recognized as legitimate players in community revitalization due to their success in attracting public funds for housing initiatives and other improvements (Marwell, 2009; Rubin, 2000). Lastly, policymakers are increasingly open to developing mutually beneficial alliances between government and nonprofits in sustainability and smart growth policy implementation (Portney and Cuttler, 2010).

In this chapter, we draw upon data collected from a sample of 134 CAAs in the US to explore how organizational and management capacities are likely to foster the success of CAAs in their pursuit of sustainability. We do this by presenting a conceptual framework that incorporates elements from strategic management theory and environmental sustainability management theory, and tests a model in which community sustainability effectiveness is explained by a range of organizational and management factors. The chapter concludes by discussing how its findings may inform broader scholarly discourse on the role of CAAs in the hollow state.

## THE POLICY CONTEXT: COMMUNITY SUSTAINABILITY

The broad concept of sustainability has many connotations for policymakers and practitioners. The World Commission on Environment and Development (WCED) first explicitly defined sustainability as "development that meets the needs of the present generation without compromising the ability of future generations" (WCED, 1987, p. 43). By considering local economic, environmental, and social characteristics when designing development projects, sustainable communities "redress the often negative or deleterious environmental and social effects of adherence to mainstream approaches to economic development" (Portney, 2005, p. 580). Although the definition of "sustainable community" varies among nonprofits, government agencies, and policymakers, many of these definitions seem to coalesce around the integration of sustainable technologies, livable communities, carrying capacity, and the expansion of economic opportunity (Agyeman, 2005; Cohen, 2011; Mayer, 1984; Portney, 2003).

Researchers have formulated several theories to explain the creation, implementation, and evaluation of community sustainability at the organizational level (Starik and Kanashiro, 2013). Such efforts have explored the causal link between environmental legitimacy and external environmental pressures (Bansal and Clelland, 2004). Other studies have explored how motivation (Bansal and Roth, 2000) and resource capability (Parisi et al., 2004) contribute to sustainability. For instance, Bansal and Roth's (2000) model of private sector ecological responsiveness suggests that competitiveness, legitimacy, and environmental responsibility are key motivators for inducing corporate ecological responsiveness. These motivators are often influenced by concern for the environment at the individual level, the degree to which organization members value the environment, and the level of interconnectedness between organization members and constituents (Bansal and Roth, 2000).

While examples of critical factors for the successful implementation of sustainability are chronicled in the business management literature, examples of antecedent conditions in community sustainability by nonprofits is not widely reported. Although operational realities of nonprofit sector agencies differ from those of private organizations, many nonprofit organizational attributes can potentially enhance performance in sustainability efforts. For example, Portney and Cuttler (2010) suggest that local governments that partner with CAAs or agencies dedicated to environmental and sustainability issues are more likely to be effective in meeting long-term sustainability goals. Recently, Berry and Portney (2013) found that the cities that included environmental organizations in the policymaking process were more likely to adopt sustainability initiatives. Moreover, nonprofit environmental groups that consider justice and equity in their planning processes are more likely to be successful in creating sustainable communities (Agyeman, 2005).

Despite the increasing importance of sustainability in the public and non-profit management literature (Portney and Cuttler, 2010; Wang et al., 2012), current management theories have not accounted for how organizational factors enhance community sustainability outcomes (Starik and Kanashiro,

2013). In fact, most managerial theories omit the importance of individual, organizational, and societal issues (Corley and Gioia, 2011) and do not consider the organization and ecosystem interdependence (Winn and Pogutz, 2013; Waddock and McIntosh, 2009) or how environmental actions influence nonprofit performance (Portney and Cuttler, 2010). The conceptual model proposed here attempts to address the theoretical and empirical limitations of past studies by identifying specific organizational and managerial capacities that enable CAAs to carry out their community sustainability goals. Unlike past studies, our focus in on the ways that organizational structure and behavior promote community sustainability outcomes and provides an organizational level perspective that assumes CAA success in community sustainability is shaped by a wide array of strategic management factors. This model utilizes a perceptual measure based on self-reports gathered through a survey of CAA managers to explain how organization-level factors influence community sustainability outcomes.

## WHAT WE KNOW: ELEMENTS OF ORGANIZATIONAL AND MANAGERIAL CAPACITIES

### Community Engagement

Community participation enhances nonprofit performance and accountability. Nonprofit organizations that integrate broad-based participation strategies and coalition building in their urban development efforts tend to be more effective (Agyeman, 2005). For example, Mayer (1984) concluded that promotion of direct resident participation in revitalization project planning and implementation increases the effectiveness of private nonprofit neighborhood organizations. Peterman (2000) asserts that local officials are responsible for ensuring neighborhood residents' voices are included in local development plans. Similarly, Hardina (2006) suggests that community-based organizations should commit to participatory techniques to achieve political power, because this increases organizational legitimacy, and access to community and stakeholder resources.

Community engagement strategies can improve public sector sustainability efforts in several ways. Portney and Berry's (2010) multivariate analysis of political and civic participation in sustainable cities revealed higher levels of civic engagement in cities pursuing sustainability goals. Thus, participatory processes that includes city residents, local elected officials, and agency officials may improve local sustainability efforts (Portney, 2005). The most common community engagement strategies used by cities are information provision activities and citizen boards (Wang et al., 2012). Also, organizations that link citizens to government institutions and adopt practices to include community members in the decision-making process may improve their organizational capacity to deliver programs and services regarding community sustainability initiatives.

## Human Resource Capacity

Achieving community sustainability requires an organizational supply of skills to understand new technology, evaluate and apply public policy, and support a stable organization. (Cohen, 2011; Portney, 2005). Nonprofit organizations can acquire these skills by drawing on the knowledge of experts, and through recruitment and training of new people. For CAAs, human resource capacity mostly centers on whether those that carry out the work of the organization have the required training and ability to meet community sustainability goals (Mayer, 1984). Managers with greater levels of educational attainment and access to training may be better positioned to create direct connections between sustainability initiatives, and the prescribed actions necessary to meet the organization's goals (Portney, 2005; Wang et al., 2012). Nonprofit leaders with such skillsets can lead the discussions about community sustainability and accurately report on organizational success in sustainability efforts. On the other hand, nonprofits struggle to gain access to outside consultants and staff training (Glickman and Servon, 1998; Mayer, 1984). Moreover, the focus on recruiting individuals with adequate expertise and distributing organizational resources for training may take away from meeting certain goals and achieving organization mission (Vidal, 1992).

Organizational capacity is positively correlated with the ability of an organization to contribute to community sustainability. Wang et al. (2012) found that organizational strategies that obtain technical expertise from experts and public managers are significantly associated with organizational capacity in sustainability. In addition, managerial capacity is an important element in cities seeking to be more sustainable (Wang et al., 2012). Thus, public managers play an important role in resource and expertise acquisition when implementing community sustainability strategies. Likewise, the skills of line managers are also important predictors of the success of sustainability initiatives (Jepson, 2003). Therefore, having skilled professional staff was expected to be positively associated with managerial perceptions of effectiveness at creating sustainable communities.

## Collaborative Networking

Nonprofit organizations often work most effectively by developing cross-sector alliances with others to bring influential decision-makers and other key stakeholders to the community sustainability process (Agyeman, 2005; Ling et al.,

2009). Several scholars have studied what motivates service delivery collaboration, such as inter-sector collaborations to provide affordable housing, create jobs, and invest in infrastructure to support community sustainability efforts (Guo and Acar, 2005; Schwartz et al., 1996; Mayer, 1984; Koontz, 2006). Others have engaged in a much broader effort to adopt various theoretical lenses for understanding drivers of cross-sector collaboration (Austin, 2000; Bryson et al., 2006; McGuire, 2006; Sowa, 2009). Resource dependency theory emphasizes how organizations enter interagency collaborations to acquire resources by decreasing resource competition with other entities (Guo and Acar, 2005). The institutionalist perspective suggests that organizations may feel pressure from funders or regulators to enter strategic alliances to increase organizational legitimacy. One study of 20 inter-agency collaborations found that resource dependence, institutional pressures, and organizational prominence were motivators for inter-agency collaboration, and organizations enter these partnerships to further enhance their competitive advantage, achieve organizational legitimacy, or reduce environmental dependency (Sowa, 2009).

Advocates of collaboration have identified many benefits of public–private partnerships (Gazley and Brudney, 2007). Among small nonprofits, collaboration with public and private entities with even informal organizational structures can lead to increased organizational capacity and highly effective programs (Takahashi and Smutny, 2001). In this same line of thinking, Selden et al. (2006), discovered that interorganizational relationships in early care and education had positive impacts on client and program outcomes. Specifically, the level of intensity for collaboration has a positive and significant effect on school readiness, staff turnover, and worker compensation (Seldon et al., 2006).

Sustainability scholars suggest that collaboration may enhance community sustainability outcomes because it provides a platform for a diverse set of stakeholders to work together and support collective actions to address sustainability concerns (Koontz, 2006; Koontz and Thomas, 2006). Moreover, collaborative environmental management may lead to successful integration of regional and local sustainability policies, and greater efficiency in achieving sustainability outcomes that cross geographical and organizational boundaries (Koontz and Thomas, 2006; Sharma and Kearins, 2011). In one study, Koontz (2006) found that local governments with lead roles in farmland preservation task forces generated positive social outcomes and enhanced social capital. Furthermore, Koontz et al. (2004) assert that numerous environmental and social outcomes are linked to the involvement of government actors. For example, their work on the role of government in collaborative environmental management found that federal and state actors made significant contributions in advancing environmental outcomes by helping to provide resources, helping organizations be innovative, providing information, and assisting with the implementation of collaborative plans. In this case, nonprofit managers can leverage collaborative relationships with government actors to enhance organizational legitimacy to meet community sustainability goals.

## Dependence on Government Funds

As the devolution of responsibility for social service delivery has shifted from federal and state governments, community-based nonprofits have taken a leading role in addressing societal issues and filling gaps in government services (Fredericksen and London, 2000). Salamon's (1995) partnership theory posits that when nonprofits are unable to provide services on a scale that is adequate enough to address social problems, government responds to this "voluntary failure" by providing additional resources to allow for greater production of welfare services. As such, public funds provide the resources for nonprofit organizations to substantially expand their operations and achieve greater levels of organizational effectiveness (Froelich, 1999). This position is supported by recent work on sustainability management, which finds that reliance on public contributions may have a significant influence on sustainable development outcomes. Cohen (2011) argues that "some of the investment in sustainable cities will need to come from public sources or at least be driven by public incentives" (p. 129). This view is also supported by recent data on US sustainability implementation revealing that more than 70 percent of cities seeking to be more sustainable rely heavily on government grants to finance their sustainability activities (Wang et al., 2012). Likewise, Koontz (2006) found that government institutions use funding, technical expertise, and human capital as resources for influencing collaborative environmental processes to improve environmental and social outcomes.

By comparison, the strategic management literature garners the most empirical support to understand how public funding may help nonprofits build capacity and carry out their mission (Glickman and Servon, 1998; Salamon, 2015). Governmental resources can contribute to organizational growth and decline (Galaskiewicz and Bielefeld, 1998). Moreover, some scholars suggest that government funding may improve CAA effectiveness by providing access to elected officials and the political process (Mayer, 1984). Similarly, tightening links with public and private donors may attract additional support for sustainability projects (Cohen, 2011). Therefore, dependence on government funding was expected to be positively associated with perceived CAA effectiveness in community sustainability.

## Revenue Diversification

Organizations with a greater number of revenue sources may be more effective in their community sustainability efforts. In fact, Cohen (2011) argues that "investment in the transformation of our cities into environmentally sustainable communities will require capital from a variety of sources" (p. 128). Recent evidence has shown that revenue diversification is an effective strategy in reducing volatility and increasing an organization's chances at survival (Carroll and Stater, 2008; Frumkin and Keating, 2011). As a result, studies on the financial vulnerability of nonprofits (Chikoto and Neely, 2014; Trussel et al., 2002) consider revenue diversification as a key indicator of financial health and of an organization's ability to withstand financial shocks. Revenue diversification allows organizations to reduce resource dependence, maintain their autonomy, and exercise greater control over their financial stability (Froelich, 1999). We may expect the same relationship about community sustainability performance and revenue diversification to exist in community-based organizations.

## DATA AND METHODOLOGICAL APPROACH

This chapter tests the relationship between organizational and managerial capacities and reported managerial perceptions of community sustainability effectiveness using online survey data obtained from the 2015 Sustainable Communities Survey that was distributed to the population of community action agencies across the US. The sampling frame represents a list of CAAs for fiscal year 2015 obtained from the Community Action Partnership national association, a membership organization that provides technical assistance and other resources to CAAs funded by the Community Services Block Grant (CSBG). The responding organizations were drawn from various cities across the US. However, a disproportionate number were located in cities of the West, East, and Midwest regions. This did not appear to be a sampling bias, because many of the CAAs on the list were located in this area. Furthermore, previous studies noted that well-established CAAs are located in these metropolitan areas (Rubin, 2000).

Data were collected via a nine-part web-based survey using Qualtrics software and designed in accordance with Dillman et al.'s (2014) tailored design method. The survey included a questionnaire with well-designed content and formatted in accordance with the latest advances in cognitive research. We pre-tested the survey with a group of experts and community-based nonprofit organization representatives, to ensure that survey questions were properly adapted for the community development audience. Initial emails with survey links were sent out in January 2015 to executive directors or chief executive officers. Survey recipients were encouraged to complete the online questionnaire and were sent additional follow-up reminder emails to encourage participation. Of the 726-survey links emailed, 134 were returned completed, resulting in a response rate of 19 percent.

## Dependent Variable

Methodologically, it is challenging to ascertain to what extent individual organizations have had an impact on community sustainability outcomes in local communities. To design and recommend policies to achieve community change can be difficult, especially considering that there is a lack of consensus among scholars on how to assess the effectiveness of CAA programs designed to improve environmental, economic, and social outcomes for people living in low-income communities (Wang et al., 2012). The difficulty in developing an accurate unitary or objective measure of the outcomes of specific sustainable development initiatives and projects has led to the adoption of several measurement strategies (Zhang et al., 2017). In testing these relationships, we use a perceptual measure to assess community sustainability effectiveness in order to tap into whether nonprofit managers believe their organization is successful in meeting community sustainability goals. We asked managers to rank on a scale of 1 to 10 "the overall effectiveness of your organization at creating sustainable communities," with 1 meaning least effective, and 10 meaning most effective.

Research suggests that self-reported data by organizational members introduce limitations through increased measurement error and bias (Stone and Ostrower, 2007). At the same time, using perceptual data to measure the effects of organizational and managerial capacities on organizational goals is not unusual in the literature (Baruch and Ramalho, 2006; Bish and Becker, 2016; Brown, 2005; Eisinger, 2002; Herman and Renz, 1999; Mitchell, 2015; Nobbie and Brudney, 2003). Moreover, Pandey et al. (2007) argue that all measures are based on perceptions, and perceptual measures may have advantages over other types of measures because they are based on the judgments of individuals who know the organization best. Mitchell (2015), likewise, argues that managers often have a clear understanding of the overall objectives, purpose, and mission of the organization, and are in the best position to develop measures to assess how the organization is achieving its goals. Based on these assertions, we contend that self-reported data by executive directors and chief executive officers provides a valid and reliable indicator for measuring the variables of interest.

## Independent Variables

The main variables of interest are measured using multiple survey items (see Table 4.1). The variable *community engagement* reflects a common community engagement strategy used by CAAs. This survey item was based on (Hardina, 2006) and was measured using a five-point Likert scale. Human resource capacity is guided by the nonprofit capacity building literature which reflects an executive director's ability to provide for the development and knowledge of staff skills (Light, 2004). This item was measured using a five-point Likert scale. In regard to collaboration, we include two dummy variables to account for whether CAA partners with local/regional and federal actors in order to meet community sustainability goals. Dependence on government funding is measured as the percentage of total revenue and revenue diversification is measured using a Herfindahl–Hirschman Index (HHI) to assess the extent CAA revenue streams are diversified.

## Other Organizational Attributes

The primary focus of this study is on community engagement, professionalization, collaboration, resource dependency, and revenue diversification associated with perceived effectiveness in community sustainability. In addition, the age of the organization, number of full-time employees, percentage of minority population, and the percentage of vacant housing, and location were also considered. Older CAAs have the experience and in-depth understanding of neighborhood needs which may enhance their ability to meet community sustainability goals. As CAAs become larger, they become more professionalized, and are able to manage a higher level of direct investment to achieve neighborhood stabilization (Cowan et al., 1999; Vidal, 1992). As such, CAAs with higher proportions of full-time staff were expected to report higher levels of perceived community sustainability effectiveness. The variable *organizational age* was measured by subtracting the year of incorporation from the year of the survey, and *organizational size* was measured as the number of full-time employees. We also control for the percentage of minority population and the percentage of vacant housing of the city in which the organization is located. Cities with a proportionally large minority population and a large percentage of vacant housing should be active in promoting a wide range of community sustainability initiatives and make a significant effort to address urban decline (Green and Fleischmann, 1991). Lastly, geographical location, or whether the organization was located in an urban area or not, was included as a control with the assumption that community sustainability strategies are likely to vary across regions. Organizational age was derived from organizational 990 forms available via Guidestar and demographic variables were obtained from the

*Table 4.1    Descriptive statistics and variable measures*

| Variable | Variable measurement | Mean | Std. Dev. | Min | Max |
|---|---|---|---|---|---|
| **Dependent variable** | | | | | |
| *Sustainable Community Performance* | Please rank the overall effectiveness of your organization at creating sustainable communities. Item scaled 1–10, with 1 = least effective, 10 = most effective. | 6.22 | 1.80 | 1 | 10 |
| **Independent variables** | | | | | |
| *Community Engagement* | Community needs and resources are fully integrated with the organization's decision-making process. Item scaled 1–5, with 1 = strongly disagree, 5 = strongly agree. | 4.22 | 0.71 | 2 | 5 |
| *Human Resource Capacity* | Staff skills are matched and up to date to ensure that projects can be delivered effectively. Item scaled 1–5, with 1 = strongly disagree, 5 = strongly agree. | 4.08 | 0.64 | 2 | 5 |
| *Federal Government Collaboration* | Organization collaborates with local government in its sustainable community endeavors. Measured 1 = organization collaborates with local government, 0 = organization does not. | 0.75 | 0.32 | 0 | 1 |
| *County/Regional Government Collaboration* | Organization collaborates with county/regional government in its sustainable community endeavors. Measured 1 = organization collaborates with county/regional government, 0 = organization does not. | 0.90 | 0.30 | 0 | 1 |
| *Government Dependence* | Percentage of the organization's budget that comes from government. | 0.81 | 0.20 | 0 | 1 |
| *Revenue Diversification* | Revenue diversification (Yan et al., 2009) $$RD = \frac{1 - \sum_{i=1}^{4} R_i^2}{0.75}$$ | 0.28 | 0.23 | 0 | 1 |
| *Age of Organization* | Age of organization in years | 46.60 | 9.80 | 3 | 94 |
| *Full Time Employees* | Number of full-time paid staff | 128.26 | 134.63 | 0 | 735 |
| *Minority Population* | Percent of nonwhite population | .40 | 2.50 | 0 | 29 |
| *Vacant Housing* | Logarithm of vacant housing | 8.81 | 1.37 | 6.17 | 12.81 |
| *Urban* | Organization is located in an urban area. Measured 1 = organization is located in an urban area, 0 = organization is not located in an urban area. | 0.22 | 0.41 | 0 | 1 |

American Community Survey (ACS). A detailed description of the measurement for all variables used in our analysis are included in Table 4.1.

## STUDY RESULTS AND NEW INSIGHTS

Multiple ordinary least squares (OLS) regression was used to test the relationships between managerial perceptions of community sustainability performance and range of organizational and management factors. Table 4.2 shows the results of the regression equation, revealing a chi-square of 5.70 with a p-value of 0.000, indicating that the combination of the eleven regressors significantly predicts the factors that promote community sustainability efforts by CAAs. The adjusted R-squared value is about 0.26. This means that nearly 26 percent of the variance in the dependent variable is explained by this model. Consistent with our first proposition, community participation in sustainability initiatives plays an important role in the development of sustainable communities. Specifically, the use of community engagement strategies by CAA managers has a positive effect on building sustainable communities. This finding suggests that executive directors of organizations see citizens as an integral part of deciding which specific programs and policies should be implemented or modified to achieve community sustainability. The implication from this finding is important for two reasons. First, it continues to expand on the limited research base that has shown the importance of community participation in fostering local sustainable development (Agyeman, 2005; Hawkins and Wang, 2012; Portney, 2005; Portney and Berry, 2010). Second, it demonstrates the need for additional research studies on why nonprofit organizations such as community-based organizations, and other informal civic sector organizations, are more likely to achieve community sustainability goals when citizens are actively involved, which would be extremely valuable to promoting citizen engagement in the development of sustainability programs for improving and protecting the quality of the biophysical environment.

One of the most critical needs in community sustainability is for CAAs to build a core of development expertise by dedicating resources to support and retain technical staff for development projects. Our findings suggest that higher investments in human resource capacity increase the probability that CAAs will produce better outcomes in their community sustainability efforts. This suggests that CAA managers are actively developing their abilities individually and collectively, which is testament to the importance of paid staff, volunteers, and board members in meeting the challenges of community sustainability.

*Table 4.2*        *Impact of nonprofit (CAA) organizational factors on community sustainability performance*

| | Community sustainability performance | | |
|---|---|---|---|
| | Coefficient | Robust SE | p-Value |
| Community Engagement | 0.478 | 0.226 | 0.036** |
| Human Resource Capacity | 0.634 | 0.227 | 0.006*** |
| County/Regional Government Collaboration | 0.995 | 0.390 | 0.012** |
| Federal Government Collaboration | 0.452 | 0.418 | 0.281 |
| Government Dependence | -2.703 | 0.725 | 0.000*** |
| Revenue Diversification | -1.920 | 0.728 | 0.009*** |
| Age of Organization | -0.008 | 0.016 | 0.587 |
| Full Time Employees | -0.000 | 0.001 | 0.765 |
| Minority Population | -0.047 | 0.020 | 0.021** |
| Vacant Housing | 0.175 | 0.106 | 0.101 |
| Urban | -0.408 | 0.273 | 0.137 |
| Constant | 2.095 | 1.823 | 0.253 |
| Observations | 134 | | |
| Prob >F | 0.00*** | | |
| R² | 0.26 | | |

*Note:* ** $p < 0.05$; *** $p < 0.01$.

The results also offer some evidence that collaborative networking is an important predictor of success in community sustainability efforts. For each additional unit of collaboration between CAAs and county/regional government, the CAA acquires greater experience with collaboration processes that help promote local community sustainability. One rationale for this finding is that CAA managers find value in county/regional collaboration because it allows for more interaction with local sustainable development experts, better coordination, and control of collaborative work. Additionally, the involvement of county and regional government actors can decrease the time needed to accomplish objectives and build community capacity to deal with the demands of sustainable development (Koontz, 2006; Koontz and Thomas, 2006). Although we find support for our proposition that county/regional collaboration increases the success of CAAs in meeting community sustainability outcomes, we do not find that collaboration between community-based organizations and federal government actors significantly increases their success in community sustainability.

We find evidence that dependence on government funding does matter to community sustainability performance. CAAs that rely on government funding are less likely to achieve significantly higher levels of community sustainability performance in the eyes of their employees. This finding is consistent with arguments on the unintended consequences of government funding (Cho and Gillespie, 2006; Guo, 2007), which suggest that reliance on public sector funding may lead to goal displacement and loss of administrative autonomy in nonprofit organizations. The irony is that, as community-based nonprofits are expected to be responsive to community needs and educate their funding sources about community sustainability issues, reliance on public sector funding might undermine their policy advocacy capacities. Findings by other scholars have also demonstrated that public sector funding may restrict nonprofit flexibility (Salamon, 1987), contribute to bureaucratization (Froelich, 1999), create accountability conflicts (Peterman, 2000; Stone et al., 2001), and decrease organizational efficiency (Gronbjerg, 1993). The results reported here indicate that reliance on government funding could negatively affect the ability of community-based nonprofits to meet their community sustainability goals and limit their societal and democratic roles.

Previous research suggested that CAAs with more diversified sources of revenue would be more likely to meet their community sustainability goals, because diversified income portfolios can decrease financial vulnerability, making a nonprofit's financial condition more stable over time. Yet, we find just the opposite: revenue diversification has a statistically significant negative effect on community sustainability performance. There are two possible explanations for this finding regarding nonprofit revenue diversification. The first is that CAA managers may be experiencing management fatigue due to an increased workload of managing various funding sources with different characteristics, which would incur high levels of transaction costs and prevent CAAs from efficiently managing fundraising and donor relationships (Chikoto and Neely, 2014; Lin and Wang, 2016). The second is the unanticipated problems associated with the effects of "crowding out" (Brooks, 2000, 2003; Nikolova, 2015). Put simply, the public's willingness to support CAA initiatives related to community sustainability may be diminished because they perceive the CAA to be well funded by government entities. Therefore, this finding can be interpreted from a resource dependence perspective, which suggests that diversification could lead to burdensome complexity and increased administrative and fundraising costs (Frumkin and Keating, 2002). Specifically, this finding provides support for earlier studies that suggest diversification as a revenue generation strategy can lead to mission drift and undermine organizational legitimacy (Froelich, 1999; Weisbrod, 1998).

Table 4.2 also shows that only one of the control variables is significantly related to community sustainability performance. CAAs located in cities with a proportionally large minority population are less likely to meet their community sustainability goals. One explanation for why areas with higher proportion of minority residents achieve community sustainability at lower rates may be the result of discrimination in environmental policymaking, and exclusionary practices that prevent minority groups from participating in the decision-making process (Agyeman et al., 2002). Moreover, federal, state, and local practices have contributed to unhealthy living conditions in low-income and minority communities, making it difficult for CAAs to engage in the range of community sustainability activities needed by distressed communities (Bradshaw, 2007).

## IMPLICATIONS AND LESSONS LEARNED

The purpose of this study was to assess empirically what organizational and management factors are related to the success of CAAs in the urban hollow state. Based on data from a survey of 134 community action agencies in the US, the regression results demonstrate that CAAs are largely effective in achieving local sustainability goals, suggesting they perform well on both traditional outcome measures and public value measures. In particular, CAAs that utilize community engagement strategies, take time to invest in human resource development, and engage in collaborative networking, are more likely to meet the demands of sustainable development. Future studies might examine whether other types of organizational and managerial factors improve community sustainability performance and to what extent.

The findings from this study have important implications for CAA managers. Organizational leaders seeking to advance local sustainable development might consider using community engagement as a public value creation mechanism to foster transformative relationships that will build sustainable communities of opportunity. CAA leaders might especially find it useful to develop participation and engagement processes that utilize local residents' knowledge and expertise for solving problems related to sustainable development. Our study also suggests that successful sustainable development will require CAAs to build a core of development expertise by dedicating resources to support and retain technical staff for development projects. When nonprofits make significant investments in human capital development the organization is better positioned to meet its goals and build the capacity of its employees. Moreover, our results indicate that CAAs' community sustainability agendas will benefit from joining forces with local and regional government actors in their areas. CAAs can collaborate with local governmental actors by pooling together resources and sharing the results of their efforts in responding to community sustainability-related issues. By working together in the pursuit of local sustainability, CAAs are able to enhance organizational efficiency, increase organizational effectiveness and drive broader social change.

While our study has shed some new light on factors that contribute to community sustainability performance, it is important to consider the methodological limitations of this study. First, the study relies on cross sectional data obtained once from executive directors of multiple community-based organizations, and therefore is limited to describing associations between variables. Performing longitudinal studies or testing these relationships in other types of nongovernmental organizations that engage in sustainability related activities can strengthen our findings. Second, this study relies on perceptual data collected through self-reported questionnaires, which may imply common method bias. The study is interested in understanding how organizational and management factors shape managerial perceptions of community sustainability performance. While perceptual data provides a broad perspective of whether or not structures and processes are believed to work on a day-to-day basis within the organization, it captures only one dimension of community sustainability performance. Future studies linking organizational and managerial factors to community sustainability performance could improve upon a measure of community sustainability by developing indicators or evaluation criteria that will allow the broadest possible coverage of components that comprise local sustainable development (Tanguay et al., 2010). Third, the organizational and managerial factors identified in this analysis do not constitute an exhaustive list of variables that may influence community sustainability performance; however, they were chosen for inclusion in this study because they represent some of the most common variables found in previous research. Despite these limitations, this analysis revealed how strategic management factors and other organizational attributes enhance CAA effectiveness in community sustainability.

These results contribute novel findings to the sustainability management literature by providing an alternative explanation to traditional management theories that disregard how organizations practices advance sustainability. To satisfy the demand for public goods in lieu of government provision, nonprofit organizations must understand how to align community sustainability goals and public value benchmarks. The role of community-based nonprofits in creating public value holds important strategic and managerial implications for organizational leaders and key stakeholders. Organized sustainable development should prioritize community engagement, requests for public funding, individual expression, community sustainability innovation, and social capital creation that reflect the transactional work in an ever-growing hollow state. Accordingly, CAAs should articulate the public value outcomes as indirect and direct benefits of their role in sustainable development.

In conclusion, community-based organizations provide crucial support to distressed neighborhoods by supporting revitalization projects and encouraging local residents to be engaged in sustainable development. This study examined the organizational and managerial capacities that influence their success in meeting community sustainability goals, as perceived by their executive directors. The use of community engagement strategy, human resource capacity, collaborative networking with county/regional governmental actors, government funding, and revenue diversification are all important predictors of community sustainability performance. CAA executive directors and other nonprofit leaders may benefit from these findings by encouraging these activities in achieving the goals of sustainable development strategies.

## REFERENCES

Agyeman, J. (2005). *Sustainable Communities and the Challenge of Environmental Justice*. New York: NYU Press.
Agyeman, J., Bullard, R.D., and Evans, B. (2002). Exploring the nexus: Bringing together sustainability, environmental justice and equity. *Space and Polity*, *6*(1), 77–90.
Agyeman, J., and Evans, T. (2003). Toward just sustainability in urban communities: Building equity rights with sustainable solutions. *ANNALS of the American Academy of Political and Social Science*, *590*(1), 35–53.
Austin, J.E. (2000). Strategic collaboration between nonprofits and businesses. *Nonprofit and Voluntary Sector Quarterly*, *29*(1 Suppl), 69–97.
Bansal, P., and Clelland, I. (2004). Talking trash: Legitimacy, impression management, and unsystematic risk in the context of the natural environment. *Academy of Management Journal*, *47*(1), 93–103.
Bansal, P., and Roth, K. (2000). Why companies go green: A model of ecological responsiveness. *Academy of Management Journal*, *43*(4), 717–736.
Baruch, Y., and Ramalho, N. (2006). Communalities and distinctions in the measurement of organizational performance and effectiveness across for-profit and nonprofit sectors. *Nonprofit and Voluntary Sector Quarterly*, *35*(1), 39–65.
Berry, J.M., and Portney, K.E. (2013). Sustainability and interest group participation in city politics. *Sustainability*, *5*(5), 2077–2097.
Bish, A., and Becker, K. (2016). Exploring expectations of nonprofit management capabilities. *Nonprofit and Voluntary Sector Quarterly*, *45*(3), 437–457.
Bradshaw, T.K. (2007). Theories of poverty and anti-poverty programs in community development. *Community Development*, *38*(1), 7–25.
Brooks, A.C. (2000). Is there a dark side to government support for nonprofits? *Public Administration Review*, *60*(3), 211–218.
Brooks, A.C. (2003). Do government subsidies to nonprofits crowd out donations or donors? *Public Finance Review*, *31*(2), 166–179.
Brown, William A. (2005). Exploring the association between board and organizational performance in nonprofit organizations. *Nonprofit Management and Leadership*, *15*(3), 317–339.
Bryson, J.M., Crosby, B.C., and Stone, M.M. (2006). The design and implementation of cross-sector collaborations: Propositions from the literature. *Public Administration Review*, *66*(s1), 44–55.
Carroll, D.A., and Stater, K.J. (2008). Revenue diversification in nonprofit organizations: Does it lead to financial stability? *Journal of Public Administration Research and Theory*, *19*(4), 947–966.

Chikoto, G.L., and Neely, D.G. (2014). Building nonprofit financial capacity: The impact of revenue concentration and overhead costs. *Nonprofit and Voluntary Sector Quarterly, 43*(3), 570–588.

Cho, S., and Gillespie, D.F. (2006). A conceptual model exploring the dynamics of government–nonprofit service delivery. *Nonprofit and Voluntary Sector Quarterly, 35*(3), 493–509.

Cohen, S. (2011). *Sustainability Management: Lessons From and For New York City, America, and the Planet.* New York: Columbia University Press.

Corley, K.G., and Gioia, D.A. (2011). Building theory about theory building: What constitutes a theoretical contribution? *Academy of Management Review, 36*(1), 12–32.

Cowan, S.M., Rohe, W., and Baku, E. (1999). Factors influencing the performance of community development corporations. *Journal of Urban Affairs, 21*(3), 325–339.

Dillman, D.A., Smyth, J.D., and Christian, L.M. (2014). *Internet, Phone, Mail, and Mixed-Mode Surveys: The Tailored Design Method.* Hoboken, NJ: John Wiley & Sons.

Eisinger, P. (2002). Organizational capacity and organizational effectiveness among street-level food assistance programs. *Nonprofit and Voluntary Sector Quarterly, 31*(1), 115–130.

Fredericksen, P., and London, R. (2000). Disconnect in the hollow state: The pivotal role of organizational capacity in community-based development organizations. *Public Administration Review, 60*(3), 230–239.

Froelich, K.A. (1999). Diversification of revenue strategies: Evolving resource dependence in nonprofit organizations. *Nonprofit and Voluntary Sector Quarterly, 28*(3), 246–268.

Frumkin, P., and Keating, E.K. (2002). The risks and rewards of nonprofit revenue concentration. *ARNOVA Annual Conference, Montreal, QC, Canada*, November.

Frumkin, P., and Keating, E.K. (2011). Diversification reconsidered: The risks and rewards of revenue concentration. *Journal of Social Entrepreneurship, 2*(2), 151–164.

Galaskiewicz, J.J., Anderson, K., and Thompson-Dyck, K. (2016). Growth and decline of community based organizations before, during, and after the great recession. *Academy of Management Proceedings, 2016*(1), 14822.

Galaskiewicz, J., and Bielefeld, W. (1998). *Nonprofit Organizations in an Age of Uncertainty: A Study of Organizational Change.* Hawthorne, NY: Aldine de Gruyter.

Gazley, B., and Brudney, J.L. (2007). The purpose (and perils) of government–nonprofit partnership. *Nonprofit and Voluntary Sector Quarterly, 36*(3), 389–415.

Glickman, N.J., and Servon, L.J. (1998). More than bricks and sticks: Five components of community development corporation capacity. *Housing Policy Debate, 9*(3), 497–539.

Green, G.P., and Fleischmann, A. (1991). Promoting economic development: A comparison of central cities, suburbs, and nonmetropolitan communities. *Urban Affairs Quarterly, 27*(1), 145–154.

Gronbjerg, K.A. (1993). *Understanding Nonprofit Funding: Managing Revenues in Social Services and Community Development Organizations.* San Francisco, CA: Jossey-Bass.

Guo, C. (2007). When government becomes the principal philanthropist: The effects of public funding on patterns of nonprofit governance. *Public Administration Review, 67*(3), 458–473.

Guo, C., and Acar, M. (2005). Understanding collaboration among nonprofit organizations: Combining resource dependency, institutional, and network perspectives. *Nonprofit and Voluntary Sector Quarterly*, *34*(3), 340–361.

Hardina, D. (2006). Strategies for citizen participation and empowerment in non-profit, community-based organizations. *Community Development*, *37*(4), 4–17.

Hawkins, C.V., and Wang, X. (2012). Sustainable development governance: Citizen participation and support networks in local sustainability initiatives. *Public Works Management and Policy*, *17*(1), 7–29.

Herman, R.D., and Renz, D.O. (1999). Theses on nonprofit organizational effectiveness. *Nonprofit and Voluntary Sector Quarterly*, *28*(2), 107–126.

Jepson, E.J. (2003). The conceptual integration of planning and sustainability: An investigation of planners in the United States. *Environment and Planning C: Government and Policy*, *21*(3), 389–410.

Koontz, T.M. (2006). Collaboration for sustainability? A framework for analyzing government impacts in collaborative-environmental management. *Sustainability: Science, Practice, and Policy*, *2*(1), 15–24.

Koontz, T.M., Steelman, T.A., Carmin, J., Korfmacher, K.S., Moseley, C., and Thomas, C.W. (2004). Governmental roles in collaborative environmental management. *Collaborative Environmental Management: What Roles for Government*, New York: Routledge, pp. 1–31.

Koontz, T.M., and Thomas, C.W. (2006). What do we know and need to know about the environmental outcomes of collaborative management? *Public Administration Review*, *66*, 111–121.

Krause, R.M. (2011). Policy innovation, intergovernmental relations, and the adoption of climate protection initiatives by US cities. *Journal of Urban Affairs*, *33*(1), 45–60.

Light, P.C. (2004). *Sustaining Nonprofit Performance: The Case for Capacity Building and the Evidence to Support It*. Washington, DC: Brookings Institution Press.

Lin, W., and Wang, Q. (2016). What helped nonprofits weather the great recession? Evidence from human services and community improvement organizations. *Nonprofit Management and Leadership*, *26*(3), 257–276.

Ling, C., Hanna, K., and Dale, A. (2009). A template for integrated community sustainability planning. *Environmental Management*, *44*(2), 228–242.

Lyth, A., Baldwin, C., Davison, A., Fidelman, P., Booth, K., and Osborne, C. (2017). Valuing third sector sustainability organizations—Qualitative contributions to systemic social transformation. *Local Environment*, *22*(1), 1–21.

Marwell, N.P. (2009). *Bargaining for Brooklyn: Community Organizations in the Entrepreneurial City*. Chicago, IL: University of Chicago Press.

Mayer, N. (1984). *Neighborhood Organizations and Community Development: Making Revitalization Work*. Washington, DC: Urban Institute Press.

McGuire, M. (2006). Collaborative public management: Assessing what we know and how we know it. *Public Administration Review*, *66*(1 Suppl), 33–43.

Mitchell, G.E. (2015). The attributes of effective NGOs and the leadership values associated with a reputation for organizational effectiveness. *Nonprofit Management and Leadership*, *26*(1), 39–57.

Nikolova, M. (2015). Government funding of private voluntary organizations: Is there a crowding-out effect? *Nonprofit and Voluntary Sector Quarterly*, *44*(3), 487–509.

Nobbie, P.D., and Brudney, J.L. (2003). Testing the implementation, board performance, and organizational effectiveness of the policy governance model in nonprofit boards of directors. *Nonprofit and Voluntary Sector Quarterly*, *32*(4), 571–595.

Osborne, D., and T. Gaebler (1993), *Reinventing Government: How the Entrepreneurial Spirit is Transforming the Public Sector*. New York: Penguin.

Pandey, S.K., Coursey, D.H., and Moynihan, D.P. (2007). Organizational effectiveness and bureaucratic red tape: A multimethod study. *Public Performance and Management Review*, *30*(3), 398–425.

Parisi, D., Taquino, M., Grice, S.M., and Gill, D.A. (2004). Civic responsibility and the environment: Linking local conditions to community environmental activeness. *Society and Natural Resources*, *17*(2), 97–112.

Peterman, W. (2000). *Neighborhood Planning and Community-Based Development: The Potential and Limits of Grassroots Action*. Thousand Oaks, CA: SAGE.

Portney, K.E. (2003). *Taking Sustainable Cities Seriously: Economic Development, the Environment, and Quality of Life in American Cities*. Cambridge, MA: MIT Press.

Portney, K. (2005). Civic engagement and sustainable cities in the United States. *Public Administration Review*, *65*(5), 579–591.

Portney, K.E., and Berry, J.M. (2010). Participation and the pursuit of sustainability in US cities. *Urban Affairs Review*, *46*(1), 119–139.

Portney, K.E., and Berry, J. (2014). Civil society and sustainable cities. *Comparative Political Studies*, *47*(3), 395–419.

Portney, K.E., and Berry, J.M. (2016). The impact of local environmental advocacy groups on city sustainability policies and programs. *Policy Studies Journal*, *44*(2), 196–214.

Portney, K.E., and Cuttler, Z. (2010). The local nonprofit sector and the pursuit of sustainability in American cities: A preliminary exploration. *Local Environment*, *15*(4), 323–339.

Rubin, H.J. (2000). *Renewing Hope within Neighborhoods of Despair: The Community-Based Development Model*. New York: SUNY Press.

Saha, D., and Paterson, R.G. (2008). Local government efforts to promote the "Three Es" of sustainable development: Survey in medium to large cities in the United States. *Journal of Planning Education and Research*, *28*(1), 21–37.

Salamon, L.M. (1987). Of market failure, voluntary failure, and third-party government: Toward a theory of government–nonprofit relations in the modern welfare state. *Journal of Voluntary Action Research*, *16*(1–2), 29–49.

Salamon, L.M. (1995). *Partners in Public Service: Government–Nonprofit Relations in the Modern Welfare State*. Baltimore, MD: Johns Hopkins University Press

Salamon, L.M. (2015). *The Resilient Sector Revisited: The New Challenge to Nonprofit America*. Washington, DC: Brookings Institution Press.

Schwartz, A., Bratt, R.G., Vidal, A.C., and Keyes, L.C. (1996). Nonprofit housing organizations and institutional support: The management challenge. *Journal of Urban Affairs*, *18*(4), 389–407.

Selden, S.C., Sowa, J.E., and Sandfort, J. (2006). The impact of nonprofit collaboration in early child care and education on management and program outcomes. *Public Administration Review*, *66*(3), 412–425.

Sharma, A., and Kearins, K. (2011). Interorganizational collaboration for regional sustainability: What happens when organizational representatives come together? *Journal of Applied Behavioral Science*, *47*(2), 168–203.

Smith, S.R., and Lipsky, M. (2009). *Nonprofits for Hire: The Welfare State in the Age of Contracting*. Cambridge, MA: Harvard University Press.

Sowa, J.E. (2009). The collaboration decision in nonprofit organizations: Views from the front line. *Nonprofit and Voluntary Sector Quarterly*, *38*(6), 1003–1025.

Starik, M., and Kanashiro, P. (2013). Toward a theory of sustainability management: Uncovering and integrating the nearly obvious. *Organization and Environment*, *26*(1), 7–30.

Stokes, R.J., Mandarano, L., and Dilworth, R. (2014). Community-based organizations in city environmental policy regimes: Lessons from Philadelphia. *Local Environment*, *19*(4), 402–416.

Stone, M.M., Hager, M.A., and Griffin, J.J. (2001). Organizational characteristics and funding environments: A study of a population of United Way-affiliated nonprofits. *Public Administration Review*, *61*(3), 276–289.

Stone, M.M., and Ostrower, F. (2007). Acting in the public interest? Another look at research on nonprofit governance. *Nonprofit and Voluntary Sector Quarterly*, *36*(3), 416–438.

Takahashi, L.M., and Smutny, G. (2001). Collaboration among small, community-based organizations: Strategies and challenges in turbulent environments. *Journal of Planning Education and Research*, *21*(2), 141–153.

Tanguay, G.A., Rajaonson, J., Lefebvre, J.F., and Lanoie, P. (2010). Measuring the sustainability of cities: An analysis of the use of local indicators. *Ecological Indicators*, *10*(2), 407–418.

Trussel, J., Greenlee, J.S., and Brady, T. (2002). Predicting financial vulnerability in charitable organizations. *CPA Journal*, *72*(6), 66.

Vidal, A. (1992). *Rebuilding Communities: A National Study of Urban Community Development Corporations*. New York: Community Development Research Center, New School for Social Research.

Waddock, S., and McIntosh, M. (2009). Beyond corporate responsibility: Implications for management development. *Business and Society Review*, *114*(3), 295–325.

Wang, X., Hawkins, C.V., Lebredo, N., and Berman, E.M. (2012). Capacity to sustain sustainability: A study of US cities. *Public Administration Review*, *72*(6), 841–853.

Weisbrod, B.A. (1998). Institutional form and organizational behavior. In W.W. Powell and E.S. Clemens (eds), *Private Action and the Public Good*, New Haven, CT: Yale University Press, pp. 69–84.

Winn, M.I., and Pogutz, S. (2013). Business, ecosystems, and biodiversity: New horizons for management research. *Organization and Environment*, *26*(2), 203–229.

World Commission on Environment and Development (WCED) (1987). *Our Common Future* [The Brundtland Report]. New York: Oxford University Press.

Yan W, Denison DV, Butler JS. Revenue Structure and Nonprofit Borrowing. *Public Finance Review*. 2009; 37(1):47–67.

Zhang, X., Warner, M.E., and Homsy, G.C. (2017). Environment, equity, and economic development goals: Understanding differences in local economic development strategies. *Economic Development Quarterly*, *31*(3), 196–209.

# 5. Bridging charitable support and public service performance: a preliminary analysis of large US city park systems

Yuan (Daniel) Cheng, Yu Shi, and Simon A. Andrew

While much has been written about the role of nonprofit organizations in the provision of public services (Behn and Kant, 1999; Alexander et al., 2010; Provan and Milward, 1995), less work has sought to understand the performance implications of relying on nonprofit organizations for financing public service provision (Cheng, 2019a; Cheng and Yang, 2019). This chapter departs from the previous ones by examining the government–nonprofit partnership from a different perspective, one in which nonprofits raise funds to support local public service systems. We are interested in finding whether nonprofit financial support improves the performance of such systems in the area of public parks. Rather than nonprofits' reliance on government financial resources, we investigate the reverse of this relationship by examining charitable spending on urban public parks and the performance of city park systems in the United States. This is an important relationship, because scholars find that nonprofits supplement financial resources and service provision, and share certain service responsibilities with public agencies, in the area of public park services (e.g., Brecher and Wise, 2008; Shi and Cheng, 2021). While we are observing a rapid growth of charitable activities and the important roles played by nonprofits in supporting public service provision, some scholars raised their concerns about the quality of services (Cheng, 2019a; Walls, 2014).

This chapter contributes to the empirical understanding of government–nonprofit relationships and public service provision in multiple ways. First, we created a dataset which combines multiple data sources, including the annual city park facts report issued by the Trust for Public Land, the Fiscal Standardized Cities (FiSC), the National Center for Charitable Statistics (NCCS) dataset and the Bureau of Census. This study investigates the correlation between charitable support and the performance of public services. Moreover, most prior studies on the performance of public services focus on output measures, such as the quantity of public services, with little emphasis

*85*

on the distributional consequences of charitable support. This study applies multiple performance indicators, such as public access to parks, to explore park system performance.

The next section of this chapter provides a brief description of the context and the theoretical framework: co-production theory. The following section describes variables, data sources, and methodology utilized to examine the relationship between nonprofit organization supporting of city parks and the performance of city park systems. Subsequent sections present a descriptive analysis and the results of the estimation of three performance models. The chapter concludes with a discussion of empirical findings, research limitations, and some directions for future research.

## THE STUDY CONTEXT: PARKS AND RECREATION

Nonprofit organizations play an important role in financing and creating public parks (Gazley et al., 2018; Pincetl, 2003; Walls, 2014). Tate Williams (2014) in *Inside Philanthropy* reported that "parks philanthropy seems to be surging," highlighting the recent increase in the number of fundraising campaigns to revitalize green open space. According to Walls (2014), private funding for urban parks has been consistently higher than public spending. Harnik and Martin (2015) presented a similar finding, which is that when estimated in per-acre terms, private park conservancies spend more than city park departments on public parks. One of the reasons for an increase in private or charitable funding is because of a general decline in federal government assistance since the Great Recession of 2008. Funding reduction from state and local governments thus may catalyze an increase in charitable giving in supporting of public parks.

An increase in charitable supporting activities may not only contribute to an improved performance of urban park systems (for example, providing amenities and facilities to park users), but it is also likely to capture the role played by nonprofit organizations in promoting civic engagement and involvement. Park conservancies and "friends of the park" groups, for example, offer platforms for citizens and residents to be engaged in the provision of local parks and recreation services (Pincetl, 2003). They provide financial resources (such as cash) for parks, and allow local communities to engage in mobilizing volunteers for trash pickup, tree planting, and trail maintenance (Madden et al., 2000). Citizens can also organize by forming "friends of the park" groups to advocate for additional public investment in urban parks. They can also participate in the development and planning for public parks (Cheng, 2019b).

The contribution of nonprofits in financially supporting urban parks can also be attributed to several factors. For example, City Parks Alliance—a national nonprofit organization that focuses on urban parks and local communities through partnerships and cross-sector collaboration—organizes its members to involve themselves in community planning, and the creation and maintenance of city parks. Public parks increase property values for surrounding neighborhoods, provide users access to nature and recreation, storm-water protection and mitigation, and water conservation. In urban areas, urban parks make cities attractive to businesses, and they make cities competitive for capital investment. Urban public parks serving more than 80 percent of urban residents can generate various forms of tangible and intangible benefits.

Local policymakers and public managers still hold reservations about the reliance of charitable organizations as sources for funding in the provision of services. Walls (2014), for example, provided several reasons for this reservation. The first reason is that the revenues received from park-supporting charities may not be stable. Also, the recreation services funded by park conservancies and friends' groups may disproportionately benefit a subgroup of the population. While the former is related to the uncertainty of funding sources, the latter is closely linked to unequal access of urban parks that generally benefits selective groups of the community. An additional reason is that an increase in the amount of private charitable donations and in support by nonprofit organizations for urban public parks are likely to result in a reduction in the allocation of public funding (Walls, 2014). The so-called "crowding-out" effect of public funding suggests that the relationship between park-supporting charities' spending and the performance of city park systems needs to be further examined.

## WHAT WE KNOW

The theory of co-production provides an important theoretical lens to understand the relationship between charitable support and public service outcomes. Co-production refers to the mix of joint activities that public service agents and citizens can develop, and thus contribute to the provision of public services (Parks et al., 1981). Brudney and England (1983, p. 63) also provided a definition, which is: "Coproduction consists of citizen involvement or participation (rather than bureaucratic responsiveness) in the delivery of urban services ... Coproduction stems from voluntary cooperation on the part of citizens (rather than compliance with laws or city ordinances) and involves active (rather than passive) behaviors." This definition highlights the importance of citizen participation and involvement.

While co-production requires the inputs of time, resources, and skills from citizens, the nature of arrangements found in co-production can take various forms (Nabatchi et al., 2017; Brudney and England, 1983). For example, individual co-production involves two entities working directly with each other with an aim to produce individual benefit; group co-production consists of a group of entities with similar characteristics working directly with each other simultaneously on a specific common concern; collective co-production involves a similar pattern of group membership as the group production, but tends to focus on spillover benefits that could benefit all members. Although previous studies tend to focus on individual citizens' role in co-producing services, the nature of service provision can be felt by members collectively (Nabatchi et al., 2017). Additionally, some scholars have suggested that institutional co-production may play an important role in encouraging and mobilizing citizen participation (Cheng, 2019b; Paarlberg and Gen, 2009).

Moreover, co-production theory assumes that citizens are voluntarily engaged to enhance the quality or quantities of the services they use (Brudney and England, 1983). For instance, citizen participation through co-production can be essential for improving the qualities of service provision. Parks and Ostrom (1999) found that small-sized police departments perform better in terms of the crime rate compared with large police departments. In smaller communities, citizens are more likely to help their neighbors watch houses when they are gone, or report suspicious activities to the police. This case indicates the co-production of local residents and the police department in the area of public safety. It also implies that the full value of public services cannot be realistically captured if citizens are not actively involved in the provision of the services.

In the context of charitable support for urban park systems, public park-supporting charities can also play important roles in engaging citizens to co-finance, co-maintain, co-manage, or co-design parks services (Cheng, 2019a; Gazley et al., 2018). According to Madden et al. (2000), the activities played by nonprofit organizations in urban park systems are closely tied to their roles in local communities and urban parks. While most volunteer organizations raise money, recruit volunteers, and perform outreach activities, large nonprofit organizations are generally involved in activities related to capital projects, landscape and design, and routine maintenance of urban parks. In other words, large nonprofit organizations tend to play a lesser role in advocacy, but more on the management of a park.

Organizations supporting public parks also play a role in advocacy for park needs in a flexible approach; that is, raising awareness of the charitable organizations' mission, encouraging residents to use the parks facilities and amenities frequently, and stimulating long-term interests and civic engagement. Other roles include outreach and programming activities; for example, managing volunteers, remedial maintenance activities such as weed removal, clean-up, visitors' information, education and outreach. While not all charitable organizations are involved in the co-production of urban parks, some are more involved in the organization and actual management of a park than others (Madden et al., 2000).

## Can Charitable Support for Urban Parks Improve the Performance of Urban Park Systems?

According to the co-production theory, the financial support provided by charitable organizations can improve the quality of public service provision via various mechanisms (Zambrano-Gutiérrez et al., 2017; Vamstad, 2012). First, co-production may increase the buy-in of citizens in government provision of public services (Zambrano-Gutiérrez et al., 2017). Involving citizens in the design and delivery of public services during the process of shared decision-making between government officials and citizens is likely to generate community trust and improve the quality of public service.

Second, co-production can encourage a diversity of ideas and inputs from citizens regarding local public good provision. The by-product of this is to bridge various ideas and local preferences to translate them into a true demand of citizens and park users. Citizens who are involved in the co-production of public services are more likely to have the opportunity to articulate their demand and shape the outcomes of public services. Zambrano-Gutiérrez et al. (2017), for example, found that more users' involvement in the core tasks of K-12 (kindergarten to 12th grade) education generates better public service outcomes in terms of students' proficiency in mathematics and English language arts. Vamstad (2012) also found a similar correlation in the case of co-operative childcare in Sweden. Parent co-operative childcare achieved a better service quality from both a user and a staff perspective (Vamstad, 2012). These empirical findings imply that the consequences of co-production to the performance of public services can be positive.

The performance of city park systems links tightly to the goals these systems serve. Parks are public places where individuals from different backgrounds can connect with each other and people can use their leisure time to enjoy nature and relieve stress. Although these dimensions are hard to assess directly. We can use various indicators to indirectly assess the performance of city park systems. First, urban parks that are located close to local residents have a positive effect on the physical activities of children. Cohen et al. (2006), for example, found that adolescent girls living less than 0.5 mile from public parks with facilities (such as playground, walking path, swimming areas) have a higher level of physical activities than those who did not have access to public park facilities. Kaczynski et al. (2008) also found that urban parks with amenities (such as streetlights, drinking fountains, picnic areas) tend to have a positive effect on children's physical activities.

The size of urban public parks also matters when assessing urban park systems. Giles-Corti et al. (2005) found that the size of public parks is associated with residents' level of usage: that is, higher level of physical activities. They argued that urban parks that are larger tend to have a relatively higher number of amenities and facilities, which provide greater satisfying experiences for park users. For example, a large urban park has attributes such as water features, trees, and natural settings. A large urban open space provides residents with a "restorative" experience, when the natural environment exposes users to a "sense of being away from their usual setting, and a sense of fascination resulting from exposure to (for example) birdlife or natural beauty" (Giles-Corti et al., 2005, p. 173). Users also reported having a higher perception of happiness, lower level of anger or aggression, anxiety, or depression (ibid.). Based on the discussion of the co-production theory and the performance of city park systems above, we hypothesize that a higher level of charitable support for city parks and recreation services is associated with a better performance of city park systems.

## DATA AND METHODOLOGICAL APPROACH

This study draws on several data sources that span from city park system characteristics, local government finance, to community characteristics. Primary data come from the annual city park facts report issued by the Trust for Public Land. The second source is the Lincoln Institute's Fiscally Standardized Cities (FiSCs) database, which contains different categories of revenues, expenditures, and debt information for the 150 largest US cities. The FiSCs database captures public spending of overlapping local governments in a given jurisdiction on various public service functions (Lincoln Institute of Land Policy, 2017). The third source is the National Center on Charitable Statistics (NCCS) Core PC files, which provides data about the expenditures and revenues of registered and reporting public charities in the US. The fourth source is the US Census American Community Survey (ACS) that provides important community-level characteristics such as race, median income, and education levels. It is important to note that we collected city park performance data of 100 major US cities in 2016, and the rest of the data for 2015, to create a time lag to allow for the time sequencing between our predictor and outcome variables in this study. After merging all these data sources for a single year, our combined data have 82 major US cities in total.[1]

### Outcome Variables: Performance

The performance of a city park system is measured by multiple indicators for 2016. They are categorized by the Trust of Public Land into three major groups:

1. Public access to urban parks, which is measured by the proportion of city residents that live within 0.5 mile of a city park. This category is an

important performance dimension of urban park system because public access to urban parks has been linked to physical activities of residents and adolescents. Access to public parks places a strong emphasis on the importance of spatial distribution of facilities, the ability of users to travel and utilize the facilities and amenities of public parks (Rigolon, 2016).

2.  Public outputs of the city park system, including a facility measure in terms of the average of per capita provision of playgrounds in parks. This category provides clues about how users' preferences can be met by local governments; that is, recreational opportunity for users to use facilities as well as satisfying different needs of users.

3.  Acreage of the city park system, including the percentage of parkland of total city area. The acreage of urban parks not only reflects the importance of green space, but it also captures economies of scope in which amenities and facilities are available to residents or park users (see Giles-Corti et al., 2005). As the percentage of parkland is highly skewed to the left, we use the log transformation of percentage of parkland as one of our key outcome variables.

The exploratory factor analysis was performed to identify whether these performance indicators can be grouped into a smaller number of factor scores to measure the overall performance of city park systems. Our results failed to converge to a single underlying factor to load all these three indicators of city park system performance (alpha = 0.349). As a result, we decided to use the above three indicators to measure multiple dimensions of park system performance.

## Predictor Variable: Charitable Support for Parks and Recreation Services

The key predictor variable—charitable support for city parks—is operationalized as total expenses of park-supporting charities in cities per 1000 population. A per capita measure is taken to standardize and rescale the charitable financial support measure. Following Cheng (2019b), park-supporting charities are identified through a combination of keyword search and the National Taxonomy of Exempt Entities (NTEE) codes. Each organization identified in the NCCS dataset is then verified through the information on their websites to ensure that the primary purpose of these charities is to support a city park. The total expenses of the park-supporting charities are aggregated at the city level to construct the total charitable support for public parks in a city in 2015.

The per capita total spending of park-supporting charities in cities ranges from a minimum value of $0 and a maximum of around $47 per resident. The mean is around $5 per resident, which is much lower than the estimated amount of public spending reported by the National Recreation and Park Association (NRPA, 2018): park recreational agency's operating expenditure of $78.26 per capita per year. This information shows that compared to public spending on parks, the financial contributions of park-supporting charities are relatively weak. However, their contributions are expected to increase over time as local governments' budgets on parks and recreation continue declining (Cheng and Yang, 2019).

**Control Variables**

As there may be factors besides charitable support that may determine the performance of city park systems (that is, public spending on parks), we include a set of control variables to account for these conditions. Drawing on existing studies of the determinants of public service performance, we include multiple control variables to represent community characteristics, government revenue structure, type of jurisdictions, and public spending on parks and recreation services. Payne et al. (2002) argued that a significant predictor of park and recreation preferences and behaviors can be the role of race. Thus, this model includes a social diversity index to measure the racial diversity of the city. It also includes homeownership rate and an index measuring community resources to explore how demographic factors and community wealth may affect park performance. Local government spending (city, county, and special districts combined) on parks and recreation services, local government own-source revenues, and whether the local government is consolidated (a dummy variable with 1 indicating consolidated) are included to control for the type of city and public investment in the city's parks and recreation services. Table 5.1 reports the detailed measures of each variable and the sources of data.

*Table 5.1*    *Variable descriptions and data sources*

| Variable name | Definition | Data source |
|---|---|---|
| Outcome variables: | | |
| *Park land* | Log parkland as a percentage of city area | Trust for Public Land |
| *Access* | Percentage population within 0.5 miles (ten-minute walk) of a city park | |
| *Playground* | Park playground per 100 000 residents in a city | |
| Predictor and control variables: | | |
| *Nonprofit spending on parks* | Per capita total expenditure of park-supporting charities in a city | National Center on Charitable Statistics |
| *Government spending on parks* | Per capita total expenditure of local governments on parks in a city | The Fiscally Standardized Cities (FiSC) database |
| *Own-source revenue capacity* | Total local government own-source revenue as a share of total local revenue | |
| *Consolidated cities* | A dummy variable, with 1 indicating consolidated cities, and 0 indicating non-consolidated cities | |
| *Community wealth index* | An index created by the factor analysis of median household income, median housing value, and the percentage of population with a bachelor's degree or higher (alpha = 0.636) | Bureau of Census |
| *Homeownership* | Homeownership rate | Bureau of Economic Analysis |
| *Population density* | Total city population divided by land area (in thousands) | Bureau of Census |
| *Social diversity index* | An index measuring the level of racial diversity in the community. It is calculated as $1 - \sum (\text{population of racial-group}_i/\text{total population})^2$ | Bureau of Census |

## Analytical Approach

An ordinary least square (OLS) model is estimated to explore the link between charitable support and the three indicators for the performance of city park systems. We test for multicollinearity with the mean variance inflator factor (VIF) and use the pairwise correlations among the regressors to ensure that a high degree of correlation does not exist between predictor and control variables. Table 5.2 provides the descriptive statistics for each of the variables in the study.

*Table 5.2　　Descriptive statistics for model variables*

| Variables | Obs. | Mean | Std. Dev. | Min. | Max. |
| --- | --- | --- | --- | --- | --- |
| Outcome variables: | | | | | |
| *Access* | 82 | 66.207 | 18.539 | 27 | 99 |
| *Playground* | 82 | 2.538 | 1.041 | 0.5 | 7.3 |
| *Percentage parkland* | 82 | 11.369 | 10.296 | 1 | 84.6 |
| Predictor and control variables: | | | | | |
| *Per capita nonprofit spending on parks* | 82 | 5.133 | 9.962 | 0 | 47.183 |
| *Per capita government spending on parks* | 82 | 172.216 | 85.396 | 46.47 | 415.97 |
| *Own-source revenue capacity* | 82 | 0.644 | 0.103 | 0.380 | 0.849 |
| *Consolidated cities (yes or no)* | 82 | 0.220 | 0.416 | 0 | 1 |
| *Community resource index* | 82 | 0.210 | 1.030 | -1.505 | 3.225 |
| *Homeownership* | 82 | 0.550 | 0.074 | 0.235 | 0.678 |
| *Social diversity index* | 82 | 0.486 | 0.117 | 0.162 | 0.708 |

*Note:* All predictor and control variables are lagged by one year in the empirical model.

## STUDY RESULTS AND NEW INSIGHTS

To answer the research question, we produce an OLS regression for each of the three main indicators of park system performance, including public access to parks, per capita number of playgrounds in parks, and percentage parkland of total city land area. Percentage parkland is transformed into the logarithmic form as the original form of the variable is heavily left skewed. Table 5.3 shows the results of the OLS regression analysis.

According to Table 5.3, our expected hypothesis of the positive correlation between charitable support and the performance of park systems is confirmed. Across those three models, there is a consistently positive correlation between the expenses of park-supporting charities and those park system performance indicators. As the expenses of park-supporting charities go up, this city's park system is likely to have increased public access to parks (statistically significant at the 0.1 level), have more playgrounds in parks (statistically significant at the 0.1 level), and have a larger share of parkland as percentage of total city land area (statistically significant at the 0.05 level). A $1 increase in the per capita total spending of park-supporting charities in a city is associated with a 0.283 percentage point increase in public access to parks, a 0.023 increase in the number of park playground per 100 000 residents, and a 1.339 percentage point increase in the percentage parkland, respectively.[2] If we change the unit of per capita spending of park-supporting charities to $1000, the substantive impact of charitable support on park system performance can be quite large. Compared to per capita local government spending on parks, the coefficients for charitable support are also larger, indicating that the per-dollar increase in charitable support for public service provision has a larger effect than the per-dollar increase in government spending. Increasing the level of charitable support for public service provision seems to be a good idea.

In addition to our findings of the positive correlation with charitable support, total spending of local government on parks is positively and statistically related to the three performance indicators of city park systems. This suggests that the involvement and support of local governments are critical to the success of city park systems. For example, model 1 in Table 5.3 shows that public access to city parks will increase when local governments have higher levels of spending on city parks. The statistically significant and positive coefficient of 0.001 on per capita government spending on parks suggests that, on average, a $1 increase in per capita local government spending on public parks is predicted to increase the proportion of total population living within a 0.5 mile of a public park by about 0.063 percentage points, all else being constant.

With regard to community wealth and demographic characteristics, the results from the community resource index show that cities with more community resources are likely to have a better city park performance. However, the level of racial diversity in a community is negatively correlated to the level of public access to parks and the number of playgrounds in parks. Homeownership has a negative and statistically significant relationship with public access to parks. These findings suggest that communities with more resources, more renters (often indicating a higher level of population density), and less racial diversity (often meaning more white population), are likely to have a better-quality city park system.

*Table 5.3*     *Impact of park-supporting charities on three measures of park system performance*

|                                         | (1)      | (2)        | (3)                         |
|-----------------------------------------|----------|------------|-----------------------------|
| Variables                               | Access   | Playground | Log percentage parkland     |
| *Per capita nonprofit spending on parks* | 0.283*   | 0.023*     | 0.013**                     |
|                                         | (0.154)  | (0.011)    | (0.005)                     |
| *Per capita government spending on parks* | 0.063*** | 0.003*     | 0.002**                     |
|                                         | (0.0210) | (0.001)    | (0.001)                     |
| *Consolidated cities (yes or no)*        | -0.316   | 0.618*     | 0.306                       |
|                                         | (5.069)  | (0.336)    | (0.268)                     |
| *Community resource index*               | 4.982*** | -0.005     | 0.245***                    |
|                                         | (1.670)  | (0.132)    | (0.068)                     |
| *Social diversity index*                 | -43.73** | -3.509**   | 0.117                       |
|                                         | (19.34)  | (1.661)    | (0.609)                     |
| *Homeownership rate*                     | -91.52***| 1.952      | 1.273                       |
|                                         | (28.69)  | (2.015)    | (1.667)                     |
| *Own-source revenue capacity*            | -54.49** | -1.147     | -0.241                      |
|                                         | (22.58)  | (1.163)    | (0.917)                     |
| *Constant*                               | 159.7*** | 3.247      | 1.057                       |
|                                         | (31.56)  | (2.184)    | (1.266)                     |
| Observations                            | 82       | 82         | 82                          |
| $R^2$                                   | 0.324    | 0.203      | 0.268                       |

*Notes:* Significance levels indicated by: * $p < 0.10$, ** $p < 0.05$, *** $p < 0.01$; two-tailed tests. Clustered robust standard errors at the state level in parentheses. All predictor and control variables are lagged by one year.

## IMPLICATIONS AND LESSONS LEARNED

This study advances our understanding of the linkage between charitable support and public service outcomes, using evidence from 82 US large city park systems. We do find preliminary evidence that charitable support for city parks can improve the performance of city park systems. By supplementing government spending and investment on public spaces, charitable support provided by friends' groups and park conservancies help public parks to be more accessible to city residents, have more facilities in parks, and develop more parkland in the city. One simple and direct conclusion may be that more financial support by citizens and nonprofits is a good thing for public service provision. City parks should explore ways to diversify their financial sources and to expand the traditional approach of financial support. However, we want to caution the readers against this simple conclusion, and we urge others to engage in further study of the performance consequences of charitable support for public service provision. While the effect of charitable support is positive, the level of charitable support for public parks is still quite low for sample cities. It may be a long way to go, or unrealistic, to rely on voluntary citizen action and nonprofit organizations for the provision of public parks. As public–nonprofit partnerships become more prevalent in the subfield of parks and recreation (Harnik and Martin, 2015; Walls, 2014), we need to closely monitor their funding interactions with local governments and their impact on public service performance (Cheng, 2019b).

This study helps researchers and practitioners better understand the relationship between the concept of co-production, charitable support for public service provision, and city park performance. While the financial contributions of these charities are certainly instrumental and may help improve the performance of city park systems, the impact of these park-supporting charities and friends' groups should be understood and analyzed beyond financial terms. Compared to the level of public spending on parks, charitable support in the form of direct expenses on parks is still small (around 1/40 based on the data we collected in this chapter). The movement of park conservancies and relying on private funding for public park management is still relatively new, and limited to a few major cities such as New York, Boston and Atlanta. Therefore, it may be too early to draw the conclusion that charitable support for public service provision is always a good thing. Also, these park-supporting charities are not just fund-raisers for their supporting public parks; they also represent a form of innovation in service delivery, allows for individual expression, creates opportunities for civic engagement and social capital building, as well as possibly civic learning and civic capacity building via engaging citizens in the process of working together with local government officials (LeRoux, 2007). These broad arrays of public values should be highlighted and promoted by local governments and park-supporting charities. By focusing on only financial contributions, local governments and charities may lose sight of the best leverage for public value creation. In the meantime, future studies should also be conducted to understand the potential equity implications of such arrangements.

Are these charities always creating public value, or will their presence compromise an equitable provision of public services (Gazley et al., 2020)? Broadening the scope of inquiry on these alternative service provision mechanisms will be critical as we further understand the role of nonprofits becoming important players in creating and financing public service provision. As more urban parks are expanding through the expansion of urban areas, the roles of nonprofits in the provision of urban park services will also be expected to grow.

Additional efforts are needed for data collection and the operationalization of variables in future studies. First, our cross-sectional data makes it very hard to draw causal claims with our findings. It may be possible that park-supporting charities are more likely to be more active in cities with a more robust city park system. There may also be omitted variable biases, as citizens' preferences for parks may make them more likely to support both public parks and park-supporting charities. Even by lagging our predictor and control variables by one year, we cannot solve all these potential problems in this study. A more dynamic understanding of the relationship between charitable support and public service performance is needed. As we continue to monitor and collect the same information about these key city park system characteristics, we may be able to discern a more robust pattern between charitable support and park performance as the longitudinal dataset is enriched. The other approach future research could take is to find innovative measures for other aspects of park performance. Fundamentally, visitation and user experiences are better measures for how a park system performs compared with the acreage or the spatial distribution of parks. Scholars have also identified ways to collect user data from participatory observations, surveys, and social media platforms (Donahue et al., 2018; Allen et al., 2001).

Future research can also shift the focus of analysis from park systems to individual park units inside or across multiple park systems. This finer level of analysis will allow us to understand the specific mechanisms of how park-supporting charities might influence park-level outcomes, such as user experiences and interaction in parks. More research should also be conducted to understand how these park-supporting charities are managed and governed to ensure both user engagement and public accountability (Cheng, 2019c). Should there be stronger public representation on the nonprofit board (Brecher and Wise, 2008)? How should government agencies and nonprofit partners design and structure their contracts or formal agreements? Whose interests do these charities truly represent? These questions are very important for us to understand the democratic and equity implications of the increasing level of charitable support for public service provision.

In conclusion, this research contributes to the conversation of the performance and accountability in the hollow state as the first few empirical studies exploring the linkage between charitable support and the performance of major urban park systems in the US. The findings and empirical strategies used in this study can be applicable to other urban and performance management contexts. The implications of this research are significant under a governance system in which governmental actors and nonprofits are jointly involved in providing public services, both via governments contracting out services to nonprofits and via direct charitable support for public service provision.

# NOTES

1.   The drop of observations is mainly due to the missing data in the process of merging multiple data sources.
2.   As the percentage of parkland is log transformed, we need to use the following formula to provide a more intuitive interpretation of the coefficient: (exp (0.0133) − 1) * 100 = 1.339.

# REFERENCES

Alexander, J., Brudney, J.L., and Yang, K. (2010). Introduction to the symposium. Accountability and performance measurement: The evolving role of nonprofits in the hollow state. *Nonprofit and Voluntary Sector Quarterly*, 39(4), 565–570.

Allen, R., Kornblum, W., and Hayes, C. (2001). *Public Use of Urban Parks: A Methods Manual for Park Managers and Community Leaders*. Washington, DC: Urban Institute.

Behn, R.D., and Kant, P.A. (1999). Strategies for avoiding the pitfalls of performance contracting. *Public Productivity and Management Review*, 22(4), 470–489.

Brecher, C., and Wise, O. (2008). Looking a gift horse in the mouth: Challenges in managing philanthropic support for public services. *Public Administration Review*, 68, S146–S161.

Brudney, J.L., and England, R.E. (1983). Toward a definition of the coproduction concept. *Public Administration Review*, 43(1), 59–65.

Cheng, Y. (2019a). Understanding nonprofit support for public services: Moving from coproduction to cogovernance. *Public Administration Review*, 79(2), 203–214.

Cheng, Y. (2019b). Nonprofit spending and government provision of public services: Testing theories of government–nonprofit relationships. *Journal of Public Administration Research and Theory*, 29(2), 238–254.

Cheng, Y. (2019c). Governing public–nonprofit partnerships: Linking governance mechanisms to collaboration stages. *Public Performance and Management Review*, 42(1), 190–212.

Cheng, Y., and Yang, L. (2019). Providing public services without relying heavily on government funding: How do nonprofits respond to government budget cuts? *American Review of Public Administration*, 49(6), 675–678.

Cohen, D.A., Ashwood, J.S., Scott, M.M., Overton, A., Evenson, K.R., et al. (2006). Public parks and physical activity among adolescent girls. *Pediatrics*, 118(5), e1381–e1389.

Donahue, M.L., Keeler, B.L., Wood, S.A., Fisher, D.M., Hamstead, Z.A., and McPhearson, T. (2018). Using social media to understand drivers of urban park visitation in the Twin Cities, MN. *Landscape and Urban Planning*, 175, 1–10.

Gazley, B., Cheng, Y., and LaFontant, C. (2018). Charitable support for US national and state parks through the lens of coproduction and government failure theories. *Nonprofit Policy Forum*, 9(4), 1–16.

Gazley, B., LaFontant, C., and Cheng, Y. (2020). Does coproduction of public services support government's social equity goals? The case of US state parks. *Public Administration Review*, 80(3), 349–359.

Giles-Corti, B., Broomhall, M.H., Knuiman, M., Collins, C., Douglas, K., et al. (2005). Increasing walking: How important is distance to, attractiveness, and size of public open space? *American Journal of Preventive Medicine*, 28(2), 169–176.

Harnik, P., and Martin, A. (2015). *Public Spaces/Private Money: The Triumphs and Pitfalls of Urban Park Conservancies.* Washington, DC: Trust for Public Land. Accessed August 4, 2016 at https://www.tpl.org/sites/default/files/files_upload/ccpe -Parks-Conservancy-Report.pdf.

Kaczynski, A.T., Potwarka, L.R., and Saelens, B.E. (2008). Association of park size, distance, and features with physical activity in neighborhood parks. *American Journal of Public Health*, 98(8), 1451–1456.

LeRoux, K. (2007). Nonprofits as civic intermediaries: The role of community-based organizations in promoting political participation. *Urban Affairs Review*, 42(3), 410–422.

Lincoln Institute of Land Policy (2017). *Fiscally Standardized Cities database.* Accessed February 22, 2017 at http://www.lincolninst.edu/subcenters/fiscally -standardized-cities/.

Madden, K., Myrick, P., Brower, K., Secunda, S., and Schwartz, A. (2000). *Public Parks, Private Partners: How Partnerships are Revitalizing Urban Parks.* New York: Project for Public Spaces.

Nabatchi, T., Sancino, A., and Sicilia, M. (2017). Varieties of participation in public services: The who, when, and what of coproduction. *Public Administration Review.* doi: 10.1111/puar.12765.

NRPA (2018). 2018 NRPA agency performance review: Park and recreation agency performance benchmarks. National Recreation and Parks Association. https://www .nrpa.org/parks-recreation-magazine/2018/april/2018-nrpa-agency-performance -review-now-available/.

Paarlberg, L.E., and Gen, S. (2009). Exploring the determinants of nonprofit coproduction of public service delivery: The case of K-12 public education. *American Review of Public Administration*, 39(4), 391–408. doi: 10.1177/0275074008320711.

Parks, R.B., Baker, P.C., Kiser, L., Oakerson, R., Ostrom, E., et al. (1981). Consumers as coproducers of public services: Some economic and institutional considerations. *Policy Studies Journal*, 9(7), 1001–1011.

Parks, R.B., and Ostrom, E. (1999). Complex models of urban service systems. In M.D. McGinnis (ed.), *Polycentricity and Local Public Economies: Readings from the Workshop in Political Theory and Policy Analysis* (pp. 355–380). Ann Arbor, MI: University of Michigan Press.

Payne, L.L., Mowen, A.J., and Orsega-Smith, E. (2002). An examination of park preferences and behaviors among urban residents: the role of residential location, race, and age. *Leisure Sciences*, 24(2), 181–198.

Pincetl, S. (2003). Nonprofits and park provision in Los Angeles: An exploration of the rise of governance approaches to the provision of local services. *Social Science Quarterly*, 84(4), 979–1001.

Provan, K.G., and Milward, H.B. (1995). A preliminary theory of interorganizational network effectiveness: A comparative study of four community mental health systems. *Administrative Science Quarterly*, 40(1), 1–33.

Rigolon, A. (2016). A complex landscape of inequity in access to urban parks: A literature review. *Landscape and Urban Planning*, 153, 160–169.

Shi, Y., and Cheng, Y. (2021). Nonprofit-as-supplement: Examining the link between nonprofit financial support and public service quality. *VOLUNTAS: International Journal of Voluntary and Nonprofit Organizations*, 32, 28–44.

Vamstad, J. (2012). Co-production and service quality: The case of cooperative childcare in Sweden. *VOLUNTAS: International Journal of Voluntary and Nonprofit Organizations*, 23(4), 1173–1188.

Walls, M.M. (2014). *Private Funding of Public Parks: Assessing the Role of Philanthropy*. Washington, DC: Resources for the Future. http://www.rff.org/files/sharepoint/WorkImages/Download/RFF-IB-14-01.pdf.

Williams, T. (2014). The new golden age of urban parks philanthropy. Inside Philanthropy. https://www.insidephilanthropy.com/grants-for-parks-gardens/2014/9/19/the-new-golden-age-of-urban-parks-philanthropy-and-its-contr.html

Zambrano-Gutiérrez, J.C., Rutherford, A., and Nicholson-Crotty, S. (2017). Types of coproduction and differential effects on organizational performance: Evidence from the New York City school system. *Public Administration*, 95(3), 776–790

# 6. Negotiating performance: the strategic responses of associations where people in poverty raise their voice

## Peter Raeymaeckers and Pieter Cools

Over the past several decades there has been a proliferation of government policies and management strategies that aim to rearrange the provision of social services by non-profit organizations (Martinelli et al., 2017; Smith, 2018). One particularly important trend is the increasing pressure for non-profit organizations to provide evidence on their performance. In most cases this pressure is exercised through performance-based contractual relations between non-profit organizations (NPOs) and their subsidizing government (Van Slyke, 2006). These contracts specify the outputs and outcomes that subsidizing bodies expect from non-profit service providers. Subsidizing public agencies may tie at least a portion of a contractor's payment as well as any contract extension or renewal to the progress that is established according to the performance indicators (Martin, 2005; Lehtonen, 2015). In this chapter we analyze the strategies adopted by a local network of NPOs in a Belgian city through a negotiating process with their subsidizing local government to determine how their performance should be measured.

A core issue in the debate of NPO performance measurement concerns the kind of evidence that must be provided as "proof" (Barman, 2007). NPOs are particularly challenged when they are mandated to prove their performance in terms of standardized and measurable output and outcome indicators to show progress in very specific and often predetermined domains of interest (Martin, 2005). This predominantly output-focused approach to NPO performance is mainstreamed by the new public management (NPM) paradigm and builds on the conviction that the scientifically legitimate production and use of performance indicators will provide a more reliable, robust, and objective information base for rational decision-making (Lehtonen, 2015; Greenhalgh and Russell, 2009; Greiling and Stötzer, 2015).

The strong belief in "objective" and measurable indicators to quantify and compare NPO performance is, however, widely criticized (Crouch, 2016), resonating with criticisms on evidence-based medicine (Greenhalgh and

Russell, 2009; RVS, 2017). Such critiques include that standardized and quantified models are not normatively neutral or objective by definition, and that these models make abstraction of the context of NPOs where they are being subjected to the expectations of several stakeholders about desirable and successful performance (Desrosières, 2014; Marée and Mertens, 2012; Lehtonen, 2015; Greiling and Stötzer, 2015). Consequently, it is argued that discussions on the types of evidence for performance of NPOs must be seen as arenas in which power and control can be both exercised and negotiated (Arvidson and Lyon, 2014; Moynihan et al., 2011). We therefore argue that looking at the various strategies that are at play when negotiating the evidence of performance is crucial for understanding the changing dynamics between NPOs and their subsidizing constituent (Bowker and Star, 2000; Arvidson and Lyon, 2014; Lehtonen, 2015). We more specifically seek to better understand the controversies that arise when NPOs are confronted with pressure from their subsidizing government to measure their performance and the strategies they use during this negotiating process.

The analysis below shows how a local network of NPOs entitled as "associations where people in poverty raise their voice" in a Belgian city strategically responds to the demand of the local government to develop a tool to measure their performance. This happens in a context where the continuation of their subsidies is openly questioned and, at least in discourse, made dependent on (proving) their performance. We use data from interviews and focus groups with coordinators, social workers, people in poverty, and representatives from the local government. Our data shows a tension between conflicting perspectives and demands from the local government on the one hand, and social professional and participants in poverty on the other. The former stresses performance in terms of evidence about results at the level of individual "clients." The latter stresses the importance of assessing the process of their participatory practices with people in poverty revolving around their participatory-group methodology and policy advocacy role. Drawing from the framework of Oliver (1991) and more recent contributions on strategic responses to institutional pressure (Pache and Santos, 2010; Arvidson and Lyon, 2014), we show how and why the NPOs in our case (tactically) comply with demand to prove their effectiveness, while using a range of tactics to introduce their own approach for performance measurement. Our analysis is particularly relevant as studies show that in European countries as in the United States, NPOs are increasingly confronted with pressure to manage their performance (Greiling and Stötzer, 2015; Arvidson and Lyon, 2014; LeRoux and Wright, 2010; Moynihan et al., 2011). By focusing on how NPOs deal with this pressure and the strategies they develop in relation to their subsidizing agency, we are able to shed more light on how performance is constructed in the complex arena where several constituents exercise different claims, while highlighting the possibility of NPOs to engage strategically in this process.

## THE POLICY CONTEXT: SOCIAL SERVICES IN THE POST-CORPORATIST WELFARE STATE

In this chapter we analyze how ELIO vzw[1] (pseudonym), a local network of "associations where people in poverty raise their voice" (APRVs) in Antwerp, deals with the demand of their subsidizing government to use a set of quantitative indicators to measure their outcomes and results. We first focus on the particular practice of APRVs and ELIO and then elaborate on the context of post-corporatist welfare states.

### APRVs: Associations where People in Poverty Raise their Voice

APRVs are considered as non-profit organizations aiming to enable people in poverty to participate as peers to the rest of society (Boone et al., 2018a, 2018b; cf. LeRoux, 2014). While there are several differences amongst APRVs, many make a general distinction between foundational work and project work. Foundational work is about being "a low threshold place where people in poverty can just be, without being judged and where we can meet and talk to people in similar situations" (Senior Participant, APRV D). Project work consists of trajectories that can go on for a few months or up to two years, in which several participants engage to work around a specific theme such as housing, mental health, or administrative simplification. At the end of a project, the group tend to communicate their results through public events and/or reports that are distributed to relevant policymakers and public administrators. Besides this, different APRVs organize and engage in a broad range of activities, including daytrips for members and their children, workshops that raise awareness about poverty, providing access to affordable means of existence, projects to lower the thresholds to participate in cultural activities, lessons on computer competencies, co-organizing the International Day of Eradication of Poverty in their region, and much more.

ELIO operates as a local umbrella or federation in the sense that it plays an important role in embedding the initiatives of the Antwerp APRVs in the institutional and policy context, developing strategies for collaboration and in coordinating and legitimizing change (Greenwood et al., 2002). ELIO has six member associations with their own coordinator and staff. Each of these associations focuses on different target groups: first-generation migrant women from Morocco and the Middle East (APRV A), "generational poor" families with young children (APRV B), older people at risk of social isolation (APRV C), people who access low-threshold support services in a certain neighborhood (APRV D), young people (APRV E), and foreign-language newcomers (APRV F). All of these APRVs are involved in a range of activities with and for people in poverty. There is intensive collaboration and regular meetings between the ELIO coordinator and the coordinators of the member associations (the six APRVs) as well as regular meetings with the social workers of the APRVs. ELIO negotiates and coordinates the yearly contracts, called "covenants," with the local government administration for this network. As part of these covenants, it has been common practice for years that NPOs were asked to provide some basic information such as the number of activities and the number of participants.

However, since 2017 the local government asked to develop measures indicating the impact and effects, meaning that it wanted information on how the anti-poverty organizations were able to improve the self-sufficiency and life conditions of individual people in poverty. This shift in focus to the measurement of impact and effects of interventions is considered as a significant evolution in management practice by both people within the administration and affected NPOs. While these contracts always included some performance indicators before, a representative of the administration stated, "these have generally not been very detailed and more geared towards proving effort than output and effects." This is now changing. According to various respondents, local scholars, and commentators, this recent change can be regarded as the next step in an ongoing evolution towards more NPM-inspired governance by the local government of our case study that has been set in motion by the previous legislation. The taken-for-granted partnership between NPOs and the local government are being replaced by a governance-by-performance approach where the local government increasingly emphasizes the importance of an NPO sector that executes public policy in a more professionalized and transparent manner (Janssen et al., 2011).

## Performance Standards in Post-Corporatist Welfare States

In Belgium, the introduction of such practice is quite new, particularly in the field of social work, and it can be regarded as a growing trend that diverges from the corporatist tradition in which the relation between governments and NPOs was characterized by longstanding partnerships, continuous negotiation, and low levels of competition between service providers (Evers and Laville, 2004; Hemerijck, 2013). Greiling and Stötzer (2015) and De Corte and Verschuere (2014) show that trust relations between NPOs and the government are characteristic of the tradition of third sector regimes in European corporatist welfare states (Evers and Laville, 2004). In these countries, such as in Austria, Germany, and Belgium, governments consider NPOs as partners that are asked to fulfil certain types of public services, in exchange for the necessary public funding. In this context the high level of trust between the government and NPOs, and the fact that the government heavily relies on the NPOs' expertise and resources, helps to explain that the latter gain autonomy.

However, some authors observe in these countries the emergence of post-corporatist government–NPO relationships where market-oriented principles are introduced (Hustinx and De Waele, 2015; Hustinx et al., 2015). As a result, government–nonprofit relationships where emphasis lies on trust and mutual agreement are increasingly replaced by a model based on performance accountability, as public departments introduce new and more performance measures to increase managerial control over the behavior of the subsidized NPOs (Hustinx et al., 2015). In this sense, Hustinx et al. (2015) show that in contrast with the close and negotiated relationship between the state and NPOs in the classic corporatist welfare state, market- and performance-oriented modes of governance are based on a less negotiated and "governance by distance" approach (Hustinx et al., 2015). Performance measures are used as instruments to increase control of the subsidizing public actor over the behavior of the NPO. Still, in European post-corporatist welfare states this evolution is happening at different speeds in various sectors, and will vary depending on the local context (Pollitt and Bouckaert, 2017).

Most local governments and NPOs have little experience of and no real performance measurement culture, given that the implementation of such NPM instruments has been relatively scarce (Pollitt and Bouckaert, 2017). The local government of our case study is known for being a frontrunner in this regard. Therefore the experiences from our case could be indicative for other NPOs that will be subjected to this institutional pressure in a context of historical corporatist state–civil society relationships.

It is argued, however, that even when NPOs are subjected to extensive external pressure by their government, a variety of tactics and strategies can be used to deal with and possibly change or resist external institutional demands (Arvidson and Lyon, 2014). Following Arvidson and Lyon (2014), we regard performance measurement and evaluation tools not only as a form of control, but also as a possible space of resistance and for promoting the values and approach of a service-providing organization. Below we present a framework to analyze the strategies that are adopted by the NPOs of this study when negotiating performance measurement with their subsidizing local government.

## Strategic Responses to Institutional Pressure

NPOs develop several strategic responses to counter and even change the demands of the subsidizing public agency, especially when they perceive that performance measures are used as a way to limit their autonomy and to control their actions (Arvidson and Lyon, 2014; Pache and Santos, 2010; Van Slyke,

2006). In this respect, Van Slyke (2006, p. 180) observed that public managers responsible for the monitoring of NPOs often know that the latter are sophisticated enough to "pull the wool over our eyes" and that NPOs can engage in different types of strategic behavior. In this chapter we draw from the work of Oliver (1991), as well as Pache and Santos (2010) and Arvidson and Lyon (2014), to identify the strategic responses NPOs can adopt in the face of governmental demands to provide evidence of their performance, particularly when they conflict with the expectations of other key constituents.

## Strategies of acceptance and avoidance

Strategies of acceptance and avoidance are considered the most passive, as organizations will not openly criticize or aim to change institutional demands. Instead NPOs will comply with or avoid the demands without trying to counter them. Oliver (1991) distinguishes between strategies of acquiescence, compromise, and avoidance. Acquiescence refers to the organizations' adoption of arrangements required by external stakeholders, and can be seen as the most passive response strategy (Oliver, 1991; Pache and Santos, 2010). Compromise differs from acquiescence as it implies the attempt to balance, pacify, or bargain with external constituents about their expectations and organizational objectives (Oliver, 1991). Compromise-seeking organizations still act in the spirit of loyalty and confirmation to the dominant values, norms, and rules, yet they actively promote their self-interests and vision. Avoidance is similar to the strategy of defensive decoupling as defined by Arvidson and Lyon (2014). They argue that a defensive meaning of decoupling refers to those strategies of organizations that show compliance with norms and performance measurement systems, while at the same time also preventing full insight to protect professional autonomy. By doing so, NPOs control the flow of information to cope with unrealistic demands of public funders.

## Strategies of (pro)active resistance

Strategies of (pro)active resistance refers to tactics aiming to change or to openly criticize institutional pressures. Strategies of manipulation are considered the most active amongst possible strategic responses. Manipulation is not a mere reaction to the power being exerted through institutional pressure; it is an attempt by the organizations on their part to exert power in order to influence expectations, change the content of institutional pressures, or to influence the very source of the institutional pressure. It is "the purposeful and opportunistic attempt to co-opt, influence or control institutional pressures and evaluations" (Oliver, 1991, p. 157). When manipulation is attempted in a way that is showing compliance with norms and procedures to an outside audience, while at the same time also preventing full insight to protect professional autonomy, Arvidson and Lyon speak of "proactive decoupling." In contrast with the aforementioned defensive decoupling, this strategy is used by NPOs that creatively try to induce changes by influencing the definition of norms (Arvidson and Lyon, 2014, p. 874; Pache and Santos, 2010). Another active strategy is defiance, which refers to the explicit rejection of at least one of the institutional demands.

Research also shows that the adoption of more active or passive strategies depends on several external factors related to the institutional environment of the respective NPO, as well as to the nature of the institutional pressure and how this is perceived by the NPO in relation to its resources and goals. An important first institutional characteristic that will determine the type of strategy refers to the diversity of multiple constituents (Oliver, 1991; Pache and Santos, 2010). When NPOs are subjected to the expectations and demands of a low diversity of constituents, few efforts are necessary to balance the low level of conflicting demands. Here, strategies such as compromising may be used to find a balance between the few stakeholders of the NPO. As a result, NPOs with multiple constituents—such as funders, the target population, and crucial partners—are more likely to develop more active strategies, especially when these demands are clearly in conflict with each other and when they touch on the essence of an organization's identity, such as its mission, goals, and core principles (Pache and Santos, 2010).

Not only do the number and diversity of constituents matter, but also the level of dependency on these constituents. Consistent with the resource dependency theory, studies have shown that when NPOs develop a high level of dependency on economic resources and/or social legitimacy from one actor, NPOs are more willing to comply to external norms and pressures, and are less inclined to develop confrontational and active strategies of resistance or manipulation because the stakes are too high (Mosley, 2012; Oliver, 1991). In this respect, a high level of control, exercised by a government that invests in several control and monitoring instruments, will enforce NPOs as agents to comply or to seek compromise rather than resistance (Greiling and Stötzer, 2015; Verschuere and De Corte, 2015; Mosley, 2012; Van Slyke, 2006).

Importantly, the use of active or passive strategies also depends on how groups within an organization perceive the pressure from the point of view of their own mission and goals (Pache and Santos, 2010). It is argued that when NPOs perceive a particular performance measurement system proposed or enforced by the government as disadvantageous for the organization in terms of social legitimacy or economic resources, they are more likely to develop active tactics of resistance by aiming to manipulate or openly criticize institutional pressures (Arvidsen and Lyon, 2014; Oliver, 1991). Earlier research shows that when performance measurement systems are introduced in the government–nonprofit relationship, NPOs often show a reaction of discomfort when questioning the norms underlying the performance systems, and when they feel that performance standards will decrease their professional autonomy (Arvidson and Lyon, 2014; Greiling and Stötzer, 2015; Hwang and Powell, 2009). As a result, NPOs will likely develop active strategies to defy, shirk, or manipulate external pressures, such as proactive decoupling or manipulation. In contrast, NPOs may be more willing to acquiesce to external pressures when the demands are compatible with their internal goals.

*Table 6.1     Semi-structured interviews with professionals*

| Date | Respondents |
| --- | --- |
| 07/03/2017 | (1) Coordinator ELIO |
| 07/12/2017 | (1) Representative Flemish anti-poverty network |
| 08/23/2018 | (1) Coordinator APRV E |
| 09/01/2017 | (1) Coordinator APRV D |
| 09/01/2017 | (2) Coordinator and social worker APRV B |
| 09/01/2017 | (2) Coordinator and social worker APRV C |
| 10/17/2017 | (2) Coordinator and social worker APRV A |
| 09/28/2017 | (1) Representative of the municipal public administration |
| 10/12/2018 | (1) Representative of large local NPO that provides social services |

The remainder of this chapter focuses on the strategies adopted by the afore-mentioned network of anti-poverty organizations called ELIO throughout an ongoing negotiating process with their subsidizing local government, to determine how their performance should be measured and which performance targets should be set.

## DATA AND METHODOLOGICAL APPROACH

Our strategy for the selection and presentation of this case study is of the "information-oriented" kind (Flyvbjerg, 2006), as we were convinced that the particular case of ELIO holds relevance for theoretical and practical questions that might be of interest to the readers of this volume. More specifically, this case offers an opportunity to take an in-depth look to the introduction and negotiation of performance measurement registration and evaluation methods for NPOs in the Belgian context.

The interviews and focus groups focused firstly on the perception concerning the cities' demand for social impact measurement and the changing relationship between the local public administration and APRVs. Second, APRV coordinators (interviews), social workers and participants (focus groups) were also asked to describe how they perceived the link (causal mechanisms) between their interventions and results and what would constitute a fair evaluation of their practices.

*Table 6.2*      *Focus groups with APRV participants and social workers*

| Date | APRV | Respondents |
|------|------|-------------|
| 09/07/2017 | B | Participants (5), Social workers (2) |
| 09/12/2017 | D | Participants (5), social workers (3) |
| 09/14/2017 | C | Participants (6), social workers (2) |
| 10/24/2017 | A | Pariticpants (9), social workers (1) |

Between June 2017 and December 2018 the authors attended 11 meetings or events (Table 6.3) where they took notes with particular attention to strategic responses to the institutional pressure. These included meetings of ELIO APRV coordinators, the ELIO board of directors, meetings with social workers on the registration of their performance, and meetings between the ELIO coordinator and representatives of the local public administration. Events included an afternoon on performance measurement organized by a local NPO platform, and two events of the municipal learning network on social impact. Importantly ELIO also organized two internal events, in December 2017 (35 participants) and November 2018 (28 participants), to present and discuss the intermediary results of the self-definition and performance registration exercises with coordinators, social workers, and people in poverty.

Using an interpretive approach to content analysis (Silverman, 2013) this data was analysed through the lenses of the literature on changing relations between state bureaucracies and NPOs, the typologies of strategic responses to institutional pressure, and the different factors influencing these responses. Below we will refer to interview data as (I: professional position of the respondent). The focus group data we will refer as (FG: description social worker or participant, APRV #) and to data from meetings as (ME: date of meeting); if needed we specify the nature of the meeting and the actor, by making a remark in the full text.

The following analysis section is structured in two main subsections. The first describes the controversies of performance measurement as perceived by the APRVs. The second part narrates the strategies used by coordinators of ELIOs throughout the ongoing negotiation with the local government about performance measurement up until December 2018.

*Table 6.3*     *Observation during meetings and events*

| Date | Type of meeting | Attending |
|---|---|---|
| 08/24/2017 | Coordinator meeting to discuss the social impact measurement exercise and approach | Coordinators APRV B, C, D Coordinator ELIO |
| 09/28/2017 | Meeting with APRV A to introduce the social impact measurement exercise and CAIMeR approach | Coordinators and two social workers APRV A, Coordinator ELIO |
| 11/08/2017 | Board of directors discussing the progress on the performance measurement exercise | 8 members of the board of directors + ELIO coordinator |
| 12/04/2017 | Project progress and feedback afternoon for all respondents and board of directors | 35 participants: 9 people in poverty, 14 social workers, 5 APRV coordinators, 5 members of the board of directors, ELIO coordinator and staff member |
| 12/18/2017 | Network day for local social service providing NPOs on social impact measurement with presentations and discussions | 30 representatives of different local NPOs |
| 03/19/2018 | ELIO board of directors discussing the progress on the performance measurement exercise | 5 members of the board of directors + ELIO coordinator |
| 04/18/2018 | Meeting with representatives of the city administration | 3 representatives of the city administration + ELIO coordinator |
| 09/03/2018 | Meeting with ELIO APRV coordinators | 5 APRV coordinators + ELIO coordinator |
| 10/23/2018 | Meeting with social workers of the different APRVs and the designers of the registration application to discuss the first version and how it would fit in their daily work | 12 social workers, 2 designers of the application |
| 11/16/2018 | Session to present the progress of the impact measurement exercise to social workers and participants in poverty | 15 people in poverty, 7 social workers, 3 APRV coordinators, ELIO coordinator |
| 11/19/2018 | Meeting with the city administration to present the progress on the new registration application | 3 representatives of the city administration + ELIO coordinator |

*Note:* CAIMeR = context, actors, interventions, mechanisms, results (Blom and Morén, 2010).

## STUDY RESULTS AND NEW INSIGHTS

### Controversies Regarding the Pressure to Measure Performance

In the 2017 covenants between local anti-poverty NPOs (including ELIO) and the local government the latter stipulated the demand to develop a "model or instrument for social impact measurement." At that point, this demand was not further specified. When confronted with this lack of clarity during a meeting with the ELIO coordinator, the responsible department's director responded that: "We are in favour of a self-confident, entrepreneurial civil society. If you are capable providers you are best placed to do this exercise yourself. If you do it rationally, I am sure we will agree on most, with the exception perhaps of some minor differences in vision" (ME: 04/18/2018)

This quote shows that the director portrays performance measurement as a rational exercise that matches an entrepreneurial attitude. However, our interviews and focus groups with representatives of ELIO reveal three types of suspicions or objections towards the expectations of the local government.

Firstly, several APRV coordinators and social workers argue that the local government is following an international management trend without a clear vision or the necessary expertise. This sentiment is echoed by one of our respondents, stating "what 'the government' expects depends very much on who you talk to at what point" (I: representative large NPO). There is no agreement on how local NPOs must develop their tools for performance measurement. Similar voices are heard during the interviews and meetings with the professionals and participants of ELIO member organizations. Among the ELIO professionals and participants many react reluctantly or even combatively when the ELIO coordinator insists that "the city says it is not clear to them what we do and what our results are" and "we have to become better in telling what we do, why and to what effect" (ME: 12/04/2017):

> I agree that we can improve how we tell our story, but on the other hand we have written dozens of reports and even handbooks over the years. They don't look at it. If they still say it is unclear what we are doing, I wonder if they really try to understand. (ME: 12/23/2018 Social Worker APRV B)

The second set of concerns relates to the perceived limits of quantitative performance registration tools. While the local government has not yet specified the method for performance measurement, the general idea is that they look for numerical indicators that would allow them to compare the performance of different service providers (I: Coordinator ELIO). Our respondents regularly emphasize that "one cannot measure everything" and that important aspects of their practice, such as participation, increasing the self-confidence of participants, and the indirect, long-term effects of their projects on policymaking, are often hard to quantify. They are wary of reducing their practice to quantitative indicators because the efforts invested in and effects of such interventions very much depend on the specific life circumstances of participants:

> When they look at our numbers some say we are not supporting enough people and that the support takes too long, but many of our participants have a very difficult background and have isolated themselves for a long time. Several other services could not help them before. For some people it can take a lot of time. (I: Social Worker APRV B)

A third often-heard suspicion is that the local government is trying to increase its control over the associations or legitimize substantial budget cuts. While never formally stated in any covenant, both the coordinators of ELIO and its members organizations and a representative of the administration are convinced that non-compliance to this demand is likely to have a negative effect on funding, while compliance will probably have effects on the goals and benchmarks of performance. During the various meetings and focus groups, several social workers expressed the fear that the local government wants to impose some indicators that do not reflect the practices and goals of the associations. Put differently, they are afraid that they will be managed "through measurement" instead of "meaning" (Norman, 2002). For example, many of our respondents are convinced that the government expects the associations to determine the performance measures in terms of labor market participation, self-sufficiency, or access to quality housing. While our respondents consider these outcomes as important to improve the situation of people in poverty, they do not agree that these outcomes can be used to assess the performance of the associations of ELIO, as they are focused primarily on advocacy and organizing very low threshold activities. Clearly the institutional demand for impact measurement is perceived as touching upon the ideological level of goal-setting, and in conflict with a view on poverty reduction that is strongly represented within the network. In this regard, we confirm Pache and Santos (2010) emphasizing that the nature of the institutional pressure in terms of targeting the functional level (means) or ideological level (goals) makes a difference. Means are generally considered to be more flexible and negotiable, while goals "are expressions of the core system of values and references of organizational constituencies and are, as such, not easily challenged or negotiable" (ibid., p. 460). Institutional demands that involve conflict at the goal level, including conflict over NPOs' autonomy to determine and pursue their own goals, are hence more likely to trigger active responses and resistance.

APRV coordinators explain the current institutional pressure within a broader evolution in the relationship with local policymakers and their administration:

> We used to be able to meet the alderman to present our proposals after a project. That does not happen anymore. They no longer want social workers and people in poverty to criticize their policy, they want silent service providers that get people off benefits as soon as possible out of poverty. This stance was already initiated by the previous, progressive coalition and has been continued by the present conservative one. (I: Coordinator APRV D)

Looking at these discussions through the lens of the typology developed by Norman (2002, p. 619), the local government generally appears as the "true believer" that encourages an increased focus "on measurement of performance." It therefore demands that effort should be put "into creating clearer, more observable measures that emphasise outcomes." Some of the coordinators, social workers, and participants of ELIO member associations, on the other hand, emerge as "active doubters" who "believe that too much emphasis on measurement gets in the way of the 'real work' of developing relationship-based work in a political environment," and they emphasize the importance of meaning over measurement. Other APRV coordinators and particularly the coordinator of ELIO take on the role of "pragmatic skeptics" by accepting that performance management becomes part of the game, and take it as a starting point to discuss the best way to do it and make sure that it also benefits its member organizations and their participants. The following subsection looks at the different strategies employed to realize this.

**Strategic Responses to the Demand for Performance Measurement**

We now elaborate on the strategies that are being adopted by the network of NPOs throughout the negotiating process with the local government. This process is stretched out over a relatively long period (mid 2017–end 2018). Using the framework of Oliver (1991) we identify three strategies that are being developed: acquiescence, compromise, and manipulation. Before elaborating on our results, we emphasize that the analysis below reflects a continuous struggle of ELIO with reconciling competing institutional demands. This means that the strategies below are often used next to each other and are often subject to trial and error.

**To acquiesce with the demands of the local government**
In first instance, the coordinators of our case study comply with the demands of the city government to develop a set of measurement indicators, for two main reasons. The first is that the financial dependency of ELIO on the local government is very high and the average member organization also receives

about 70 percent of its income from covenants with the local government via ELIO. Confirming Oliver's (1991) assumption that high levels of financial dependency lead towards passive strategies of acquiescence, coordinators explain that there were no alternatives to compliance with the demand of the city government; or as the ELIO coordinator puts it during the interview, "if we do not act on this now, we will be on the chopping block." Secondly, while the coordinators generally agree with the concerns described above, most of them also recognize the need and opportunity to be more reflective and able to communicate clearly about their performance (Arvidson and Lyon, 2014). This need is particularly tangible in this case because people within the city administration often complain that APRV social workers "do nothing more than drinking coffee and talking with the same people in poverty for years" (I: Coordinator ELIO). Several professionals and members of the board of directors therefore recognize the need to become better in explaining the value and performance of their practice (ME: 11/08/2017; 12/04/2017; 10/23/2018).

### Seeking a compromise within the network and in relation to the local government

Situated between conflicting expectations from the active doubters amongst its professionals and people in poverty, and the apparent true believers in the city administration, the ELIO coordinator presents himself as a pragmatic skeptic (Norman, 2002) seeking to satisfy both sides. We learn from the literature, however, that a compromise is difficult when faced with conflicting demands about goals, especially when actors within the organization have a stake in the discussion (Pache and Santos, 2010).

Interestingly, the choice of ELIO to organize an internal participative process around performance measurement appears crucial to enable a compromise both within the network and in relation to the local government. On several occasions, coordinators, social workers, and participants were invited by ELIO to explain what they were doing, which practices they developed, why, and which effects this should have under particular circumstances. It also organized a workshop where these actors were asked to formulate indicators and methods for data collection that can be used to measure their performance (ME: 12/04/2017). We observed that this participatory approach enabled stakeholders within the organization to clearly formulate the essence of what they are doing. This enhanced the willingness of the "active doubters" to find a way to better capture and communicate their performance, which is a key aspect of the city department's demand (I: Representative City Department).

The internal exercise resulted in a shared stance of the ELIO network on performance measurement, which the coordinator uses and defends in negotiations with the local government and in discussion with other partners (ME: 12/18/2017; 04/18/2018). More specifically, the participative process with social workers, people in poverty and coordinators of ELIO resulted in a perspective on performance assessment where focus lies not only on the measurement of results and outcomes, but also on identifying and explaining the difficult process of reaching, engaging, and working with people in poverty. As already stated, the social workers of the APRVs of ELIO were very much concerned that a narrow approach to performance measurement, only focusing on outputs, would fail to reward the many efforts they conduct to organize low-threshold activities and to build a trusting relationship with people in poverty. Social workers and people in poverty thus argued that any effort to assess performance should also provide explanations on how the practices of the associations lead to these results. More specifically, two recommendations were formulated to measure the performance of their practices. First, the respondents of ELIO emphasized that any assessment of their performance should include all voices of all relevant constituencies, especially the voice and perspective of people in poverty. Second, they also stated that the success of their practices and activities is very much dependent on the context of their target group, defined as the life circumstances and the problems people in poverty face in different life domains such as housing, financial well-being, education, and childcare. These respondents often refer to the "complex web of problems" people in poverty are confronted with. Subsequently, the respondents of ELIO argued that an assessment of performance should take these contextual factors into account.

Based on these recommendations the ELIO coordinators started to build their own vision of performance assessment. To this end they used insights from scientific and academic work, putting forward a broad perspective emphasizing the importance of a shift from a narrow perspective on performance measurement where focus only lies on using output indicators, towards a broader perspective on evidence-based practice where focus lies on "what works, for whom and under which circumstances" (Blom and Morén, 2010; Boost et al., 2017). The importance of the question of "for whom" is argued by using studies putting forward a democratic approach where the assessment of performance is constructed in a dialogue between all relevant stakeholders (Vandenbroeck et al., 2012). They also used insights from studies such as Blom and Morén (2010) and Boost et al. (2017) emphasizing the importance of looking at the particular context that could explain the success of specific interventions. This contextual and democratic approach to assessing NPO performance could, according to the coordinators, lead to better answers that are able explain the impact of practices of NPOs working with very vulnerable target groups such as people in poverty. This view is captured by the following quote that became a kind of mantra of the ELIO coordinator: "We received the question 'what works', from the City. Ok that is fair enough, but in return we posed another question: what works for whom, under which circumstances?" (ELIO coordinator).

In relation to the local government it appears that ELIO's active and visible engagement to develop its own performance measurement tool increases its weight to negotiate its own approach on the measurement of performance (ME: 11/19/2018). For instance, the 2018 covenant states that ELIO has to track the trajectories of 40 of its participants in the context of the performance measurement exercise. The network was not willing to track people's individual trajectories. Instead it argued that throughout its participatory exercise on performance measurement, it involved more than 40 people in poverty in multiple focus groups and brainstorm sessions, which it considers as subsequent moments, "trajectories" of data collection. The city department accepted this interpretation as it was convinced that the ELIO network is able to develop its own measurement system. By gaining recognition for its participative approach, ELIO arguably improved its position to influence the definition of norms on which its impact will be measured and assessed. Next, we analyse how the coordinators used this opportunity to change the expectations of the government by using tactics of manipulation.

**Manipulation as influencing indicators and evaluation criteria**
In the context of strategic organizational responses, manipulation is to be understood as "the purposeful and opportunistic attempt to co-opt, influence or control institutional pressures and evaluations" (Oliver, 1991, p. 157). In our case, ELIO's strategy is not about aiming to control the opposition through domination or co-opting opponents. Its tactics are about influencing the values, definitions, and criteria of desirable performance that will underpin the registration and evaluation of its practices in the future.

The efforts to manipulate the expectations and demand of the government are observed when analyzing the discussion between the local government and the ELIO network concerning the use of the self-sufficiency matrix. This matrix aims to scale the self-sufficiency of "clients" of public health care and social services. Developed in the United States, it reached Belgium via the Netherlands, where it is promoted by consultancy agencies and implemented in some services of the larger Dutch cities. At several meetings, the public department's director proposed ELIO to implement the so-called "self-sufficiency matrix" in order to grasp its effectiveness of poverty reduction in terms of increasing people's ability to take care of their own. As time progressed, government representatives who closely follow up ELIO's efforts increasingly emphasized this matrix as the preferred tool. However, we have already mentioned above that the network contested the relevance of the measurement of self-sufficiency, as this output measure does not take into account the many efforts to organize low-threshold activities and efforts to build a trust relation with the vulnerable target group. As an alternative, the ELIO coordinators put forward their own broader approach on performance and evidence, which is more sensitive to their goals and process by focusing more on the group and structural dynamics of poverty reduction over individual ones.

Several tactics were used to convince government representatives of their approach on performance measurement. One of these strategies concerns the writing and distributing of elaborate reports where the coordinators draw from insights from academic publications and experts to formulate their own approach to the measurement of performance. Above, we have already elaborated on the scientific expertise the coordinators use to broaden the approach to performance measurement by emphasizing the question of "what works, for whom and under which circumstances" (Blom and Morén, 2010). Furthermore, ELIO started the implementation of a mobile application to register its practice at the level of its foundational work and project work. Simultaneously, an internal working group has been initiated to discuss possible ways to register data about individual trajectories without damaging trust or weakening the focus of the APRVs on advocacy and group activities. In its present version the registration focuses on the participation of people in poverty on the group level, and structural poverty reduction as defined by the network.

By adopting these strategies the ELIO coordinators claim their own expertise. They mobilize external scientific expertise and programmers of mobile applications trying to take the driver's seat for determining the indicators and criteria of their performance. As such, they raise the bar for the local government if it was to impose another registration tool or dispute their approach, making it harder for government representatives to impose their values and definitions of key concepts. We emphasize that these tactics cannot be defined as "avoidance" or decoupling (Arvidson and Lyon, 2014) because the ELIO coordinators are not obfuscating what they are actually doing. On the contrary, a high level of transparency, while being watched closely by the public department, is important to maintain their legitimacy. Rather than keeping government officials in the dark, one could argue that ELIO tries to actively shape the implementation of performance measurement and perhaps even overwhelm the officials with its expertise and clear vision.

The success of this strategy can be explained by the fact that ELIO was able to capitalize upon a lack of knowledge and expertise in the local government's demand, which allowed it to creatively reinterpret expectations and terms such as participation, trajectories, and empowerment. For now, there has not been any significant reduction in local public subsidies, nor has the network been assigned to perform tasks that are perceived to be in conflict with its goals and mission.

Our study provides several new and relevant insights for NPOs in European countries and the United States. It also shows that NPOs are struggling with the challenge to provide evidence on their performance for their multiple constituencies (Smith, 2018). This chapter develops the case study of ELIO to shed light on how a local network of anti-poverty organizations strategically responds to the institutional demand for performance measurement in the country of Belgium where such management tools are relatively new, particularly in the field of social services. The ELIO network provides public value by building trust relations with people in poverty and constructing safe spaces where people in poverty meet, connect, and gain the opportunity to discuss with policymakers the needs they face on several life domains.

More specifically this case highlights how the network deals with conflicting institutional demands from the local government, and from professionals and participants inside its own organization, who can be designated as true believers and active doubters of performance measurement, respectively (Norman, 2002). Interestingly, our chapter shows that while ELIO coordinators initially accept the government's demand to provide proof of their results and outcomes, we observe that, in the subsequent dialogue with government representatives, the coordinators of ELIO attempt to shape and influence the terms and conditions used to measure their performance by using active strategies of manipulation. This finding differs from the evidence put forward by other studies showing that when NPOs are enforced to prove their evidence using performance indicators, they engage in strategies of "deflection" (Blom and Morén, 2010), "decoupling" (Arvidsen and Lyon, 2014), or "tactical mimicry" (Dey and Teasdale, 2016). These strategies imply that organizations say one thing to their subsidizing constituent and act in a very different way in everyday practice. In contrast, we found that the compliance of ELIO to the governments' demand is not disingenuous: it is negotiated, and made dependent on whether the performance tool can serve its organizational goal without losing autonomy. Our results confirm the importance of the negotiating process that precedes the implementation of a performance system, and suggest that NPOs can influence this process by proactively strategically engaging in this process by claiming their expertise and suggesting performance measurement tools that fit their practice. NPOs should therefore invest in capacity-building on how performance can be measured. We showed that when NPOs increase their knowledge on expertise by using scientific expertise on performance measurement they can actively increase their agency in the negotiating process with their subsidizing agent. The coordinators of our case, for example, contested the narrow output-focused approach of the government by using scientific studies, while arguing that any attempt to measure performance should elaborate on key questions such as the question of "what works, for whom and under which circumstances" (Blom and Morén, 2010; White, 2009; Boost et al., 2017). The fact that ELIO actively tried to change the institutional expectations also contradicts the assumption made by Oliver (1991) that in a context where NPOs are highly dependent on the subsidizing actor who develops a high level of control, NPOs will stick to passive strategies of resistance such as acquiescence. In contrast, the coordinators heavily relied on the perspective of their internal constituents. They defended a stance on performance measurement that was based on the perspective of social workers who were afraid that a narrow approach focusing on outputs would conceal the many efforts they conduct to build a trust relationship with people in poverty. This result resonates with findings of Pache and Santos (2010) who argue that when understanding the behavior of NPOs faced with conflicting institutional demands, one also has to take into account that the extent to which one or more sides of the conflict are represented within the organization will determine the nature of the response.

## IMPLICATIONS AND LESSONS LEARNED

An important key lesson that explains ELIOs provisional success to influence the expectations on how to measure performance was the lack of clear vision and expertise among representatives of the government. Building on their participative process with internal constituents, and drawing on academic literature on performance measurement and social impact, the ELIO coordinator was capable to provide convincing answers about which approach to performance measurement was best suited for their practice and goals. To explain this finding, we need to look at the particular context of post-corporatist welfare states where NPO–government relations are gradually and slowly moving away from the corporatist tradition in which local governments tended to invest in trust relationships and sustainable relationships with NPOs (Hustinx et al., 2015). Because the implementation of performance-based management is still relatively new in these countries, organizations such as ELIO seem to have opportunities to shape the development of these practices.

When governments are still looking for the best ways to implement such management practices locally, NPOs can claim and mobilize expertise and present themselves as a pragmatic and sceptic actor to influence these debates and instruments to their advantage. We confirm research emphasizing that the process of determining indicators and benchmarks is an important sociopolitical arena. Indicators and measurement tools are performative in the sense that they materialize the NPO–government relationship and shape future practice (Bowker and Star, 2000; Arvidson and Lyon, 2014; Lehtonen, 2015). From this perspective, our case study might indicate a window of opportunity for service-providing NPOs and for practitioners to be actively engaged in shaping how performance measurement will be done in the near future.

We follow Ebrahim (2019), who argues that decisions about how to conduct impact evaluation should be based on a careful analysis of the local context and the organization's specific practices and goals. More specifically, in our case, coordinators preferred a broad perspective on impact evaluation by adopting a realist evaluation approach (Boost et al., 2020). Such an evaluation approach allows organizational members to build a program theory where interventions are carefully described, workable principles are analyzed that explain how and to what extent interventions are able to reach results, and short-term and long-term outcomes are identified (Boost et al., 2020). This analysis can be used to improve organizational learning on how to improve interventions and practices to realize rights of vulnerable target groups, but also to find ways to measure outcomes in the long term.

It has to be recognized that our research holds limits beyond the difficulty to generalize our findings from this highly contextualized case study. By focusing on the demand for performance measurement, we have not paid attention to other evolutions in the field of service provision in this Belgian city or its broader region (Smith, 2018). The evolution towards performance measurement does not happen in a vacuum, and a focus on related trends might have deepened our understanding of the conflicting institutional demands challenging ELIO and similar service providers. Also, by focusing predominantly on how the institutional pressure was perceived by those active within ELIO, we might have presented a somewhat one-sided picture of the local government's institutional demand and the intentions behind it.

We encourage future research to study not only the implementation but also the negotiation of performance measurement instruments as a way to analyze changing governance relationships. In order to understand how the provision of services is evolving, we propose that particular attention is paid to the agency of NPOs to shape these performance measurement instruments throughout a strategic process of balancing conflicting expectations from their multiple constituents. From this perspective, our study indicates a window of opportunity for service-providing NPOs in both European welfare states and the United States that are being challenged by their subsidizing constituency to be actively engaged in shaping how performance measurement will be done in the near future. In conclusion we emphasize that NPOs need to invest in developing a process- and context-oriented approach on evidence-based practice, to make visible the impact of their interventions by answering key questions such as what works, why, and under which circumstances (Blom and Morén, 2010).

## NOTE

1.   "VZW" is short for *Vereniging Zonder Winstoogmerk*, a Dutch title that refers to the network organization's juridical status as a non-profit organization. Henceforth we will refer to this organization as ELIO.

# REFERENCES

Arvidson, M., and Lyon, F. (2014). Social impact measurement and non-profit organisations: compliance, resistance, and promotion. *Voluntas*, 25, 869–886. https://doi.org/10.1007/s11266-013-9373-6.

Barman, E. (2007). What is the bottom line for nonprofit organizations? A history of measurement in the British voluntary sector. *Voluntas*, 18(2), 101–115.

Blom, B., and Morén, S. (2010). Explaining social work practice—the CAIMeR theory. *Journal of Social Work*, 10(1), 98–119. https://doi.org/10.1177/1468017309350661.

Boone, K., Roets, G., and Roose, R. (2018a). Social work, poverty and anti-poverty strategies: creating cultural forums. *British Journal of Social Work*. http://hdl.handle.net/1854/LU-8552380.

Boone, K., Roets, G., and Roose, R. (2018b). Social work, participation, and poverty. *Journal of Social Work*. http://hdl.handle.net/1854/LU-8552379.

Boost, D., Cools, P., and Raeymaeckers, P. (2017). Handvatten voor de ontwikkeling en evaluatie van lokaal sociaal beleid: het CAIMeR-model. In: Raeymaeckers, P., Charlotte Noël, Didier Boost, Caroline Vermeiren, Jill Coene and Sylvie Van Dam (eds), *Tijd voor sociaal beleid. Armoedebestrijding op lokaal niveau* (pp. 153–167), Leuven: ACCO.

Boost, D., Raeymaeckers, P., Hermans, K., and Elloukmani, S. (2020). Overcoming non-take-up of rights: a realist evaluation of integrated rights-practices. *Journal of Social Work*. https://doi.org/10.1177/1468017320948332.

Bowker, G.C., and Star, S.L. (2000). *Sorting Things Out: Classification and Its Consequences*. Cambridge, MA: MIT Press.

Cools, P., and Raeymaeckers, P. (2017). *Sociale impactmeting bij Verenigingen Waar Armen het Woord Nemen: Een toepassing op basis van het CAIMeR model. Rapport van Fase 1*. Antwerpen: Universiteit Antwerpen Faculteit Sociale Wetenschappen.

Crouch, C. (2016). *The Knowledge Corrupters: Hidden Consequences of the Financial Takeover of Public Life*. Cambridge: Polity Press.

De Corte, J., and Verschuere, B. (2014). A typology for the relationship between local governments and NPOs in welfare state regimes: the Belgian case revisited. *Public Managment Review*, 16(7), 1011–1029.

Desrosières, A. (2014). Statistics and social critique. *Partecipazione e Conflitto: The Open Journal of Sociopolitical Studies*, 7(2), 348–359

Dey, P., and Teasdale, S. (2016). The tactical mimicry of social enterprise strategies: acting "as if" in the everyday life of third sector organizations. *Organization,* 23(4), 485–504.

Ebrahim, A. (2019). *Measuring Social Change: Performance and Accountability in a Complex World*. Stanford, CA: Stanford University Press.

Evers, A., and Laville, J.L. (eds) (2004). *The Third Sector in Europe*. Cheltenham, UK and Northampton, MA, USA: Edward Elgar Publishing.

Flyvbjerg, B. (2006). Five misunderstandings about case-study research. *Qualitative Inquiry,* 12(2), 219–245.

Greenhalgh T., and Russell J. (2009). Evidence-based policymaking: a critique. *Perspectives in Biology and Medicine*, 52(2), pp. 304–318. doi: 10.1353/pbm.0.0085.

Greenwood, R., Suddaby, R., and Hinings, C.R. (2002). Theorizing change: the role of professional associations in the transformation of institutionalized fields. *Academy of Management*, 45(1), 58–80. https://www.jstor.org/stable/3069285.

Greiling, D., and Stötzer, S., (2015). Performance accountability as a driver for changes in nonprofit–government relationships: an empirical insight from Austria. *Voluntas*, 26(5), 1690–1717. 10.1007/s11266-015-9609-8.

Hemerijck, A. (2013), *Changing Welfare States*. Oxford: Oxford University Press.

Hustinx, L., and De Waele, E. (2015). Managing hybridity in a changing welfare mix: everyday practices in an entrepreneurial nonprofit in Belgium. *Voluntas*, 26(5), 1666–1689.

Hustinx, L., De Waele, E., and Delcour, C. (2015). Hybridization in a corporatist third sector regime: paradoxes of "responsibilized autonomy." *Voluntary Sector Review*, 6(1), 115–134.

Hwang, H., and Powell, W.W. (2009). The rationalization of charity: the influences of professionalism in the nonprofit sector. *Administrative Science Quarterly*, 54(2), 268–298. https://doi.org/10.2189/asqu.2009.54.2.268.

Janssen, P. Cantillon, B., and Vandenbroucke, F. (2011). *Voor wat hoort wat: Naar een nieuw sociaal contract*. Antwerpen: De Bezige Bij.

Lehtonen, M. (2015). Indicators: tools for informing, monitoring or controlling? In: Jordan, Andrew J. and Turnpenny, John R. (eds), *The Tools of Policy Formulation: Actors, Capacities, Venues and Effects. New Horizons in Public Policy* (pp. 76–99). Cheltenham, UK and Northampton, MA, USA: Edward Elgar Publishing.

LeRoux, K. (2014). Social justice and the role of nonprofit human service organizations in amplifying client voice. In Austin, J.M. (ed.), *Social Justice and Social Work: Rediscovering a Core Value of the Profession* (pp. 325–338). Los Angeles, CA: SAGE.

LeRoux, K., and Wright, N. (2010). Does performance measurement improve strategic decision-making? Findings from a national survey of nonprofit social service agencies. *Nonprofit and Voluntary Sector Quarterly*, 39(4), 571–587.

Marée, M., and Mertens, S. (2012). The limits of economic value in measuring the performance of social innovation. In: Nicholls A., and Murdock, A. (eds), *Social Innovation* (pp. 116–134). London: Palgrave Macmillan.

Martin, L.L. (2005). Performance-based contracting for human services. *Administration in Social Work*, 29(1), 63–77. DOI: 10.1300/J147v29n01_05.

Martinelli, F., Anttonnen, A., and Mätzke, M. (2017) *Social Services Disrupted: Changes, Challenges and Policy Implications for Europe in Times of Austerity*. Cheltenham, UK and Northampton, MA, USA: Edward Elgar Publishing.

Mosley, J.E. (2012). Keeping the lights on: how government funding concerns drive the advocacy agendas of nonprofit homeless service providers. *Journal of Public Administration Research and Theory*, 22(4), 841–866.

Moynihan, D.P., Fernandez, S., Kim, S., LeRoux, K.M., Piotrowski, S.J., Wright, B.E., and Yang, K. (2011). Performance regimes amidst governance complexity. *Journal of Public Administration Research and Theory*, 21, 141–155.

Norman, R. (2002). Managing through measurement or meaning? Lessons from experience with New Zealand's public sector performance management systems. *International Review of Administrative Sciences*, 68(4), 619–628.

Oliver, C. (1991). Strategic responses to institutional processes. *Academy of Management Review*, 16(1), 145–179.

Pache, A.-C., and Santos., F. (2010), When worlds collide: the internal dynamics of organizational responses to conflicting institutional demands. *Academy of Management Review*, 35(3), 455–476. doi:10.5465/AMR.2010.51142368.

Pollitt C., and Bouckaert G. (2017), *Public Management Reform. A Comparative Analysis—Into the Age of Austerity* (4th edn). Oxford: Oxford University Press.

RVS (2017). Zonder context geen bewijs: Over de illusie van evidence-based practice in de zorg. Raad voor Volksgezondheid en Samenleving. https://www.raadrvs .nl/documenten/publicaties/2017/06/19/zonder-context-geen-bewijs (accessed September 1, 2019).

Silverman, D. (2013). *Doing Qualitative Research: A Practical Handbook*. London: SAGE.

Smith, S.R. (2018). The future of nonprofit human services. *Nonprofit Policy Forum*, 8(4), 369–389.

Van Slyke, D.M. (2006). Agents or stewards: using theory to understand the government–nonprofit social service contracting relationship. *Journal of Public Administration Research and Theory*, 17(2), 157–187.

Vandenbroeck, M., Roets, G., and Roose, R. (2012). Why the evidence-based paradigm in early childhood education and care is anything but evident. *European Early Childhood Education Research Journal*, 20(4), 537–552.

Verschuere, B., and De Corte, J. (2015). Nonprofit advocacy under a third-party government regime: cooperation or conflict? *Voluntas*, 26(1), 222–241.

White, H. (2009). Theory-based impact evaluation: principles and practice. *Journal of Development Effectiveness*, 1(3), 271–284. doi:10.1080/19439340903114628

# 7. Reconceptualizing performance: filling the hollow state with public value

### Kelly LeRoux and Nathaniel S. Wright

While the centralization of government reached its zenith in the 20th century, decentralization and the rise of a market-based orientation have thus far dominated the 21st century approach to governance (Langer, 2018). Globalization, fragmentation of political authority, and persistence of "wicked problems" creates a need for governments to work across political and sectoral boundaries to design effective policy solutions and public services. Alternative modes of public service delivery through contracting, grants, vouchers, and co-production have been widely embraced by policymakers of all parties as a way to accommodate the myriad and particularistic service demands of an increasingly diverse electorate, tap into innovative program designs, and enhance political optics by limiting growth of the government workforce. In light of these realities, the hollowing out of government is likely to continue well into the future. Thus, the question we must now center our debate around is: How are we to maximize the performance of a hollow state? How do we ensure that governments design their service delivery partnerships with private organizations in ways that produce the best value for the public?

Although the answers to these questions require continuous pursuit, the chapters in this book collectively point to a need to reconceptualize definitions of performance in the hollow state to account for public value creation. Traditionally, performance in outsourced service delivery has been defined by the extent to which programs and services produce the desired result. As such, they are largely outcome-oriented as the focus is on achieving predetermined or intended goals. Yet, as the studies in this book highlight, there are important process elements associated with outsourced service arrangements that help to create public value, despite being overlooked in conventional assessments of performance. Sometimes public value is achieved by providing opportunities for civic learning, expression of citizen voice, expanded freedom and service choices for citizens, promoting inclusive participation, or the creation of social capital when individual citizens engage in voluntary collective action in the pursuit of community improvement or public good. Thus, "good" performance of a government partner organization (or set of organizations) cannot be measured solely by outcomes, but must also be measured by processes that create public value, promote democratic citizenship, strengthen bonds of community, and foster a civil society.

In the remainder of this chapter, we distill the key lessons we hope that readers will take away from this book. First, we argue for the need to adopt a holistic view when assessing the performance of the hollow state. A holistic view is one that integrates traditional measures of outcomes, impact, and effectiveness with measures of public value creation. We examine each study in the book according to this holistic approach and discuss the capacity of specific policy instruments to generate public value. Along the way, we highlight consistencies these studies show with regard to promoting the accountability and performance of nonprofits as hollow state actors. We also highlight consistencies in the evidence with regard to challenges including capacity issues, funding insecurity, and government disinvestment, which create performance obstacles. Finally, we discuss implications for government organizations contracting with nonprofits or otherwise partnering with these organizations for improving monitoring and designing performance measures. We also discuss roles for individual citizens, including specific ways they can engage with nonprofit organizations to help improve accountability and performance and contribute to public value.

## A HOLISTIC VIEW OF PERFORMANCE IN THE HOLLOW STATE: INTEGRATING OUTCOMES WITH PUBLIC VALUES

We propose a new way of assessing hollow state performance that weds traditional outcome measures with "specific, identifiable content" of public values (Bozeman, 2007). For the purpose of assessing the cases presented in this book, we use five of the six[1] elements of Moulton and Eckerd's (2012) nonprofit sector role index as measures of public value expression: innovation, advocacy, individual expression, social capital creation, and citizen engagement. We include one additional measure of public value offered by Bryson et al. (2014), which is civic learning and civic capacity-building.[2] We are not suggesting these are the only public values that government–nonprofit partnerships might yield, or the only ones that we should look for when evaluating these arrangements. Other partnerships between government and private providers might generate additional types of public value, and it is incumbent upon public managers to identify such value when it is created, so as to maximize this value in the design of future service delivery arrangements.

When we integrate both traditional measures of performance (outcomes) with a public values perspective, the cases presented in this book reveal a complex picture of performance in the hollow state. In these studies, non-profits acting as government partners sometimes fall short on traditional performance measures. Yet even when they fail to achieve their intended program or service outcomes, these government–nonprofit service arrangements create public value in a variety of ways that contribute to community-building, allow for individual expression, and foster civic engagement. Table 7.1 summarizes each public service "case" (study) examined in this book, along with the policy tool highlighted by the case, and how the case measures up in terms of outcomes, as well as various forms of public value creation.

In the case of public education, Ford's study (Chapter 2) shows that nonprofit schools do not perform as expected on traditional outcome measures, as school closure is not determined by student performance. Nonprofit schools can be low-performing when measured by student test scores, but they continue to operate due to the state's laissez-faire approach to the city's education market. The policy tool introduced in this case is vouchers, which allow low-income citizen-parents to act as "customers" who "vote with their feet" and spend their public education dollars on the school of their choice, including private nonprofit and religious schools. In theory, this sort of competition should drive all schools in the city to perform better on measures such as student test scores, as schools try to signal their quality to potential customers. The voucher program assumes that parents will "shop" among competing schools, gather information, compare options, and enroll in the school of their choice. For this system to work effectively, parents must select the schools with the best outcomes (student test scores) and punish those with lowest scores by leaving, ultimately forcing the school out of business. Yet no such consequence exists for the nonprofit schools in this case. Ford's study shows no significant relationship between reading and math proficiency and reduced closure rates, although those with greater total school enrollment, start-up status, and annual growth do have reduced closure risk. Putting pressure on the school to perform better falls entirely to the citizen–parent "customer," as there is no mechanism for the state department of education to terminate a school from the voucher program for its low academic performance. While we would consider this case as failing to meet traditional measures of performance as defined by program outcomes, this case highlights the use of vouchers as an instrument that can create public value. Vouchers represent an innovative form of service delivery in that they provide an alternative to public provision. They also provide an outlet for freedom of choice and individual expression. Low-income citizens, who vouchers are designed to benefit, may feel powerless by their lack of choices and may not have the option to move to another jurisdiction that offers

*Table 7.1    A holistic approach to evaluating performance: outcomes achieved + public value creation*

| Case | Traditional Performance Measurement: Intended Outcomes Achieved | Public Value Creation | | | | | | |
|------|------|------|------|------|------|------|------|------|
| | | Innovation | Advocacy | Individual Expression | Social Capital Creation | Citizen Engagement | Civic Learning/ Civic Capacity-Building |
| Public Education *Policy tool: Vouchers* | No | Yes | No | Yes | No | No | No |
| Public Health *Policy tool: Contracting* | Some | Yes | No | No | No | No | No |
| Local Sustainability *Policy tool: Grants and Contracting* | Yes | Yes | No | Yes | Yes | Yes | Yes |
| Public Parks *Policy tool: Co-production* | Yes | Yes | No | Yes | Yes | Yes | Yes |
| Social Welfare: *Policy tool: Contracting and Co-production* | Yes | Yes | Yes | Yes | Yes | Yes | Yes |

better public services. Vouchers that allow for personal choice is one way to help citizens feel empowered and to have agency in personal decision-making.

In the case of public health, Zhao and LeRoux's study (Chapter 3) shows that service contracting in the context of public health is more often than not linked to improved community health outcomes. In this case, contracting ranks high on traditional measures of performance as intended health outcomes— reduction in sexually transmitted infection, reduced teen birth rates, and reduced tobacco use—are largely achieved, but the use of contracting as a policy tool in this context generates little in the way of additional public value creation. This case highlights in many ways the benefits that can be achieved from contracting when conditions are optimal, and when managers are strategic about what they outsource. It is important to note that local public health departments contract with private providers for only a small percentage of total services. The findings from this study suggest that managers are highly selective and strategic about the services they outsource, and tend to contract out only for those services they know can be successfully outsourced. For example, outsourcing services with low transaction costs (easy to measure) such as HIV/STD testing and treatment is statistically linked to a lower rate of STIs in the community; and pregnancy prevention services are linked to overall lower rates of teen births in the community. At the same time, there is minimal public value creation apparent in this type of hollow state arrangement. Contracting represents an innovation in the sense that it offers an alternative to bureaucratic service delivery, but it offers little else in the way of individual expression, social capital creation, engaging citizens, civic capacity-building, and other measures of public value.

Wright and Reames (Chapter 4) showed us a dimension of the hollow state in which nonprofit community action agencies (CAAs) are tasked by the federal government, as well as local governments, with carrying out local sustaina-bility initiatives. CAAs are the nation's largest federally funded vehicle for addressing causes and conditions of systemic poverty in low-income commu-nities. As the authors point out, however, these organizations have expanded their service scope in recent years well beyond affordable housing, job train-ing, and education, to include implementation of sustainability initiatives such as residential weatherization, energy conservation, and transportation. As their case demonstrates, nonprofit CAAs are largely effective in achieving local sustainability goals, suggesting that these organizations perform well on tra-ditional outcome measures as well as public value measures. In some ways, it is unsurprising that CAAs' implementation of sustainability initiatives checks nearly all the boxes of public value creation. CAAs originated from 1960s and 1970s War on Poverty funding and carried a federal mandate for "maximum feasible participation" which embedded strong participatory norms into these organizations that have endured long beyond the mandate. These organizations also have a strong tradition of advocacy and efforts to politically mobilize and empower marginalized communities. Consistent with these traditions, Wright and Reames find that CAAs in their study adopt practices to include community members in the decision-making process, which improves organizational capacity to deliver programs and services regarding community sustainability initiatives. An interesting insight offered by their study is that government funding is linked to organizational effectiveness in achieving community sustainability initiatives. At the same time, revenue diversity is linked to greater accomplishment of community sustainability initiatives. Moulton and Eckerd (2012) suggested that government funding transfers public value to nonprofits, including advocacy. Yet we see a tension in this case, in that revenue diversity "buys" CAAs a degree of autonomy from government, allowing them to speak against government policies they oppose, whereas CAAs that rely entirely or primarily on government funding may find their advocacy that contributes to the achievement of sustainability goals is stifled.

Turning to the case of local public parks, Cheng, Shi, and Andrew (Chapter 5) illustrate how co-production might be used as a policy tool to improve performance. In this case, co-production assumes the form of citizen-led park-supporting charities including "friends of the parks" programs. These organizations not only work to raise money to supplement public park budget expenditures for equipment and capital projects, but also to bring voluntary labor in improving park grounds, clean-up, providing visitor information, programming, and so on. Citizens form these groups in order to help co-finance, co-manage, co-maintain, and co-design local public parks. Using three key measures of outcomes—acreage, access, and playgrounds per capita—Cheng and his colleagues show that park-supporting nonprofits generally help to achieve these outcomes. Thus, parks-supporting nonprofits perform well on traditional measures of performance, but simultaneously create unmistakable public value. These nonprofits provide a vehicle for local citizens to volunteer, socialize, deliberate, advocate, and work to better their community. They help to build trust among community members, and provide a space for civic learning and engagement, as citizens can play a direct role in the planning of one small part of their community. These park-supporting charities also provide opportunities for citizens to discuss wants and needs, gain insight into public budgets and local spending, and learn to better articulate service demands. For these reasons, nonprofit "friends of" groups formed specifically to support public organizations might be particularly beneficial in creating public value, even if in some instances they fall short of achieving their intended outcomes. Generally speaking, it is best to think of these government–nonprofit partnerships as "public value-added" or a supplement to government service provision, rather than a substitute.

The final case examined in this book, by Raeymaeckers and Cools (Chapter 6), is set in the Belgian context and involves a federated organization with six member associations whose mission involves minimal service delivery, but rather is geared toward advocacy and political empowerment of six specific groups at high risk of poverty (immigrants, elderly, etc.). These member organizations are known as "associations where people in poverty raise their voice" and are classified as anti-poverty organizations whose goal is to improve self-sufficiency and life conditions of individual people in poverty. To this end, they engage in a variety of activities including "daytrips for members and their children, workshops that raise awareness about poverty, providing access to affordable means of existence, projects to lower the thresholds to participate in cultural activities, lessons on computer competencies, co-organizing the International Day of Eradication of Poverty in their region, and much more." Raeymaeckers and Cools describe how this federation of organizations faced pressure from their sponsoring government to demonstrate impact through measures of individual member self-sufficiency. Historically, it had been sufficient for associations to report in the aggregate how they had helped address issues of poverty, and funding principals were satisfied with reports that progress was made. But, the funding sponsor began to demand new performance reporting that required data on the long-term outcomes or trajectory of service recipients. Through in-depth qualitative research, Raemaekers and Cools demonstrate how the managers of these nonprofits engaged in strategic responses to these institutional pressures, and were ultimately successful in deflecting these demands and negotiating what gets reported to government funding agencies. Consistent with the findings of Wright and Reames, this case reveals that government funding has a suppressing effect on nonprofits' advocacy roles and constrains their ability to give voice to their clients' needs. In this case, Raemaekers and Cools demonstrate how skilled managers strategically employ their professional expertise to manipulate the demands in their favor. They describe how associational managers "actively shape the implementation of performance measurement and perhaps even overwhelm them [government officials] with [their] expertise and clear vision."

We would rate this case as largely successful in achieving traditional measures of performance, as it accomplished its intended goals. At the same time, the nonprofits examined in this case exude public value. They are not only advocating on behalf of several identity groups living in or at risk of poverty, but they are also providing civic education to their members in an effort to strengthen civic capacity and democratic participation. Moreover, these associations provide a collective space for these citizens, all of whom experience marginalization, to interact and engage in dialogue, debate, and planning on behalf of the associations. In this way, the associations both build social capital by strengthening bonds among members, but also function as schools of democracy by training members for active engagement in the political process.

As we pointed out in Chapter 1, nonprofit performance is inherently multidimensional and thus cannot be reduced to a single metric or measure. Our argument here is consistent with that notion, in that we advocate for a more holistic approach to evaluating performance in the hollow state by accounting for both traditional outcome measures and public value creation. Reliance on traditional outcomes measures alone obscures the intangible "social good" and value created by nonprofits in other ways. While governments and other funders should expect public value to be created in their partnership arrangements with nonprofits, they should at the same time continue to push nonprofits to work toward producing demonstrable program outcomes. We see these approaches to evaluating nonprofit performance as complementary, and it is important for funding agencies to negotiate with private organizational partners both the outcome measures, as well as which types of public value creation they will be held to account for.

## CHALLENGES FOR NONPROFITS

Collectively, these chapters have highlighted a number of challenges for nonprofits in their roles as partners to government in delivering public services. Challenges faced by nonprofits in these studies include capacity issues, government disinvestment, revenue diversification, constraints on nonprofit organizational autonomy, lack of clear performance expectations, and the challenge of maintaining accountability to multiple stakeholders.

The increasing precarity of government funding has forced many nonprofit partners in the hollow state to diversify their revenue portfolio, creating the problem of being an agent to many different principals. Nonprofit partners in public service may be receiving funding not only from government, but at the same time from private foundations, corporations, federated organizations such as United Ways, individual donors, user fees, as well as generating their own income from commercial ventures. The need to respond to this diverse set of stakeholders at times creates conflicting demands of nonprofit managers. For example, Wright and Reames describe how nonprofit managers may be experiencing management fatigue as the result of the increased workload associated with managing various funding sources. It is not uncommon for nonprofit managers to have performance measures imposed on them from government funders, and a different set of performance reporting requirements for their foundation funding, for United Way to require a logic model, along with the need to create annual reports and periodic communications to share with donors. In Chapter 1, we discussed the many challenges associated with various types of performance measures and the impossible task of choosing the "best." We have also discussed how the lack of clear performance expectations even from a single funder can create ambiguity and reduced accountability, as Ford demonstrates with the case of public education. The point we are trying to make here is simply that these issues are compounded by the increasing budgetary fragmentation experienced by nonprofits.

A related challenge of course is that most nonprofits operate on an extremely thin margin of administrative overhead, and performance measurement in many instances equates to an unfunded mandate. The market-based ethos pervading both the public and the nonprofit sector in recent years means that nonprofits are expected to do more with less, including designing and implementing sophisticated systems for assessing and conveying their impact. Yet, the vast majority of nonprofits lack the staffing capacity and professional expertise to do this well. The reality faced by most nonprofits is one in which employees (particularly administrators) perform multiple roles, and competing demands on their time force a scenario in which the minimum required to stay in compliance is what gets measured. Nonprofits are rarely given adequate funds to support the performance measurement or data collection that is expected of them. Government organizations, along with other institutional funders that partner with nonprofits in public service delivery, should scale their performance reporting expectations to match what they can compensate the organization to deliver.

Reliance on government funding also creates some unintended consequences for nonprofits with regard to performance. The cases presented in both Chapter 4 and Chapter 6 show how government funding leads to organization "capture" of nonprofits, hampering their ability to carry out their advocacy roles. The more dependent that nonprofits are on government for their revenue, the riskier they may feel it is to speak out against policies or practices the organization objects to, even if it is to give voice to the needs and interests of clients served by the organization. Given that nonprofits are uniquely suited to providing interest representation for marginalized groups and those who often go voiceless in the political process (LeRoux, 2009), this is an important public value created by nonprofits, and yet government funding has a detrimental effect on advocacy. The value of advocacy and political empowerment work generally gets overlooked in the calculus of nonprofit performance (unless the organization's primary mission is advocacy), which is unfortunate, as it is one of the distinctive virtues of nonprofits and an important contribution to a pluralist, democratic society.

Another unanticipated consequence of government funding is that it may complicate nonprofits' ability to raise revenue from other sources, which has become increasingly necessary in recent years. Put simply, the public's willingness to support nonprofits may be diminished because they perceive service-providing nonprofits to be well funded by government. This "crowding out" effect has been well documented elsewhere (Brooks, 2000, 2003), but it is worth mentioning here as it compounds the problem of resource scarcity for nonprofits, and of their ability to generate the organizational slack needed to devote to performance questions. Government funding may create other unintended consequences for nonprofits, including goal displacement and loss of administrative autonomy (Cho and Gillespie, 2006; Guo, 2007). The irony is that as community-based nonprofits are expected to be responsive to community needs and educate their funding sources about issues in their respective service policy domains, reliance on public sector funding undermines their policy advocacy capacities. Findings by other scholars have also demonstrated that public sector funding may restrict nonprofit flexibility (Salamon, 1987), contribute to bureaucratization (Froelich, 1999), create accountability conflicts (Stone et al., 2001), and decrease organizational efficiency (Gronberg, 1993).

Historically, scholars have argued that government funding enhances the "publicness" of nonprofit organizations (Salamon, 1995; Moulton and Eckerd, 2012), and indeed there is evidence that government funding shapes nonprofit behavior in some ways that public values such as equity, social capital building, and emphasis on citizen participation and participatory governance are realized (LeRoux, 2009; Moulton and Eckerd, 2012). However, given that earned income is the fastest-growing share of nonprofit revenue, and nonprofit budgets are increasingly comprised of diverse income streams, these long-standing assumptions are called into question. Evidence presented in some of our cases suggests that in fact government funding may inhibit the expression of public values in some instances, such as providing interest representation for marginalized citizens. Advocacy furthers the public value of equity in that nonprofits speak on behalf of those whose voices are left out of political decisions, including public budgeting priorities. Yet, many nonprofits face constraints in their advocacy roles, even if a minority of their funding comes from government; they are often risk-averse and reluctant to "bite the hand that feeds them."

Should we expect nonprofits only to embrace public values in proportion to their reliance on government finding? The answer of course is no, but we must also recognize that nonprofits have inherent qualities and organizational behaviors that contribute to social good, and some of this production of social good would occur completely independently of government funding. Some of the very features that make nonprofits attractive collaboration partners for government—flexibility, innovation, advocacy, responsiveness to unique populations and problems, ability to fundraise—have become stifled by regulatory burdens and performance expectations associated with government funding. The answer is to this problem is not less government funding for nonprofits, but a reconceptualization of nonprofit performance. Not only does this require a rethinking of conventional academic wisdom and theories about the impact of government funding on nonprofit behavior and values, but it also requires public managers who oversee nonprofit partnerships to think differently about how they define and reward performance of their nonprofit service delivery partners. Accounting for public value creation alongside traditional outcome and output measures is one way.

## IMPLICATIONS FOR NONPROFIT FUNDERS: GOVERNMENT, FOUNDATIONS, AND CITIZEN DONORS

Milward and Provan (2000) suggested that accountability in the hollow state requires a principal–agent relationship so that the legal authority of government can be used to impose expectations on service providers. While the legal authority of public organizations remains critical, the principal–steward model proposed by Van Slyke (2006) offers a more accurate depiction of the relationships that exist between most public organizations and their nonprofit partners. The principal–steward model starts from the assumption that nonprofits are trustworthy and have good intentions. As such, relationships are between government contract managers and nonprofit profit administrators are more collaborative, governed by communication, mutual respect, and negotiated expectations. With regard to performance measurement issues, public managers should in most cases adopt the principal–steward model. Public managers must embrace a holistic view of performance, evaluating nonprofits on the achievement of both clearly identified program outcomes as well as public value creation. Nonprofits generate immense public value, but it can be difficult to quantify. Nonprofits acting as partners to public organizations generally do not get credit for public value creation in the calculus of their contract renewals or grant awards. To the extent public managers think about, or give weight to the value added benefits nonprofits bring beyond their service delivery, it may be only in the abstract. We argue that public values are a necessary complement to traditional performance metrics, and public managers and other institutional funders should account for public value creation in their assessment of nonprofit performance.

The process of determining which performance measures an organization will be evaluated against should be mutually negotiated between the funding organizations and nonprofit, should allow for adjustment at regular intervals, and should take into account the reality that many of the services nonprofits provide are inherently difficult to measure. As Raymaeckers and Cools demonstrate, nonprofits can influence this process by proactively and strategically engaging with their funding principals, by invoking their professional expertise and suggesting performance measurement tools that fit their practice. Despite the many challenges associated with measuring outcomes, they remain important, and nonprofits should be encouraged to strive for demonstrable program outcomes. Organizations that can speak in outcomes and results will be better positioned to compete for corporate dollars, wealthy private donors, and venture capitalists. Having the ability to message about outcomes can have significant benefits for nonprofits. Capturing outcome measures can help nonprofits in their marketing efforts, in strengthening their relationship with current stakeholders, and in conveying their record of performance to current and prospective clients, donors, volunteers, and board members.

Citizens also have an important role to play in holding public organizations and their hollow state service delivery partners accountable. In several cases throughout this book, we see the effects of citizens in performance outcomes. Reames and Wright show how racial minorities drive nonprofit CAAs toward greater success in achieving local sustainability goals, and Cheng, Shi, and Andrew show how the community's education level shapes demand-making for more park acreage, access, and playgrounds. Raemaeckers and Cools show how organizational constituents affected by poverty can be mobilized to speak out on behalf of a reform that poses a threat to organizational resources. Parents served by school choice vouchers in Ford's study could in theory be highly effective in pressuring schools to perform better, but they often lack the education and information needed to hold poor-performing schools accountable. In many cases, citizens lack the knowledge of "who is in charge" or how to exert influence. To this end, nonprofits with program designs that have built-in opportunities for civic learning, civic capacity-building, dialogue, and deliberation are ideal, promoting democratic citizenship and increased prospects for broader civic participation. These are highly valuable program features that nonprofits are uniquely suited to perform, and should thus be encouraged to every extent possible by those who fund the work of nonprofit organizations.

The chapters presented in this book also have implications for both institutional funders and as well as individual donors with regard to supporting nonprofit overhead. Nonprofits cannot be expected to invest time in collecting data or building performance measurement capacity without commensurate resources. There have been numerous social media campaigns in recent years criticizing nonprofit directors' salaries, and urging donors to withhold contributions from organizations with higher overhead costs. Anomalies notwithstanding, nonprofits generally act as good stewards of their gifts by investing in capacity that helps the organization grow, improve the quality of its staffing and service, and extend its mission to more people. Donors must look past administrative ratios, and resist the temptation to ask how much of their dollar is going toward "the cause." The notion that we can neatly separate nonprofit administrative expenditures from the mission it carries out is an antiquated idea that must be abandoned. At the very least, donors should look at a three-year average for administrative spending, and even better, ask how the organization has made an impact or created value. Another effective strategy for holding these organizations accountable is to get personally involved. Citizens who are regular donors to an organization whose mission they care about can inquire about ways to become more directly involved, through volunteering, or joining an advisory board or the governing board.

Foundations and government funders should also follow this guideline and resist imposing artificial or unrealistic administration-to-program ratios on their grantees and contractors. For their part, nonprofit managers must remain sensitive to donor perceptions, and maintain respect for the past abuses that have created such a negative connotation for overhead. At the same time, nonprofit managers need to invest in capacity and consistently strive toward demonstrating both outcomes and extrafinancial value, if they are to success-fully position their organizations to succeed in this increasingly competitive environment.

## FINAL WORDS

There is a tendency to perceive something that is hollow as being fragile or susceptible to destruction. The notion of a hollow state has at times been portrayed through an ominous lens, projecting a spiral of descent for American bureaucracy. These concerns are not entirely invalid, given the prospects for failures of accountability. And yet, a hollow state need not be one that rests on the verge of fracture. Public organizations must maintain the infrastructure necessary for responsible vetting of service partners and ongoing oversight of their performance. Public managers must consider what they most need to accomplish in service delivery partnerships—whether it is efficiency, effectiveness, equity, or responsiveness—and accept that it is impossible to maximize all of these objectives simultaneously. Public managers must determine which is most important in any given scenario, and select service delivery partners accordingly. In short, a hollow state need not be fragile, if it is filled with expressions of public value. We hope that this work will push the field toward a reconceptualization of performance, and promote practices that fortify the hollow state through intentional effort and design of service delivery arrangements in ways that encourage maximum expression of public values.

## NOTES

1. The sixth element of "service delivery" applies to all of the cases examined in this book.
2. We acknowledge there is a good deal of overlap between Moulton and Eckerd's six value expressions and Bryson et al.'s (2014) public values expressions which include citizens acting as problem-solvers or co-creators actively helping to define what is valued by the public, instances of civic learning and/or building civic

capacity, and instances of citizens shaping policy through dialogue and deliberation. We use Moulton and Eckerd's as the primary measures of public value, since theirs is the earlier of the two works.

# REFERENCES

Bozeman, B. (2007). *Public Values and Public Interest: Counterbalancing Economic Individualism.* Washington, DC: Georgetown University Press.

Brooks, A.C. (2000). Is there a dark side to government support for nonprofits? *Public Administration Review*, 60(3): 211–218.

Brooks A.C. (2003). Do government subsidies to nonprofits crowd out donations or donors? *Public Finance Review*, 31(2): 166–179.

Bryson, J.M., Crosby, B.C., and Bloomberg, L. (2014). Public value governance: Moving beyond traditional Public Administration and the New Public Management. *Public Administration Review*, 74(4): 445–456.

Cho, S., and Gillespie, D.F. (2006). A conceptual model exploring the dynamics of government–nonprofit service delivery. *Nonprofit and Voluntary Sector Quarterly*, 35(3), 493–509.

Froelich, K.A. (1999). Diversification of revenue strategies: Evolving resource dependence in nonprofit organizations. *Nonprofit and Voluntary Sector Quarterly*, 28(3), 246–268.

Gronberg, K.A. (1993). *Understanding Nonprofit Funding: Managing Revenues in Social Services and Community Development Organizations.* San Francisco, CA: Jossey-Bass.

Guo, C. (2007). When government becomes the principal philanthropist: The effects of public funding on patterns of nonprofit governance. *Public Administration Review*, 67(3), 458–473.

Langer, J. (2018). Organizational identity and the nature of stakeholder relationships in the blended age of organizing. Unpublished dissertation, UIC Library Theses Database, retrieved on April 7, 2021 from https://indigo.uic.edu/articles/thesis/Organizational_Identity_and_The_Nature_of_Stakeholder_Relationships_in_the_Blended_Age_of_Organizing/10798223.

LeRoux, K. (2009). Paternalistic or participatory governance? Examining opportunities for client participation in nonprofit social service organizations. *Public Administration Review*, 69(3): 504–517.

Milward, B.H., and Provan, K.G. (2000). Governing the hollow state. *Journal of Public Administration Research and Theory*, 10(2): 359–379.

Moulton, S., and Eckerd, A. (2012). Preserving the publicness of the nonprofit sector: Resources, roles, and public values. *Nonprofit and Voluntary Sector Quarterly*, 41(4): 656–685.

Salamon, L.M. (1987). Of market failure, voluntary failure, and third-party government: Toward a theory of government–nonprofit relations in the modern welfare state. *Journal of Voluntary Action Research*, 16(1–2): 29–49.

Salamon, L.M. (1995). *Partners in Public Service: Government–Nonprofit Relations in the Modern Welfare State.* Baltimore, MD: Johns Hopkins University Press.

Stone, M.M., Hager, M.A., and Griffin, J.J. (2001). Organizational characteristics and funding environments: A study of a population of United Way-affiliated nonprofits. *Public Administration Review*, 61(3): 276–289.

Van Slyke, D. (2006). Agents or stewards: Using theory to understand the government–nonprofit social service contracting relationship. *Journal of Public Administration Research Theory*, 17(2): 157–187.

# Index

academic performance 5, 33, 38, 127
acceptance, strategies of 107
accountability 25, 31–2, 38, 45, 67, 135
    fragmentation of 3
    measure of 18
    mechanisms 14–15
    of nonprofits 39, 126
    and performance 3–4
    reduced 133
ACS *see* American Community Survey
    (ACS)
active doubters 114–15, 119
administrative spending 136–7
adult population 54–6
advocacy 16, 33, 77, 88, 103, 118, 126,
    130–31, 134
Affordable Care Act 44
Agbodzakey, J. K. 47
Alchian, A. A. 48–9
Aldridge, R. 16
American Community Survey (ACS)
    74–5, 90
Andersson, F. O. 29, 32–3
Andrew, S. 20
anti-poverty organizations 105, 119, 131
APRVs *see* associations where people in
    poverty raise their voice (APRVs)
Arvidson, M. 106–8
asset specificity 48, 50
associations where people in poverty
    raise their voice (APRVs) 104–5,
    109
    on advocacy 118
    coordinators 112, 114
    social workers 112, 115
attainment 28–9, 68
autonomy 59, 71, 79, 106–7, 113, 119,
    130, 132, 134
average asset specificity 50–52
avoidance, strategies of 107

Bansal, P. 66
Barman, E. 6–7
Benjamin, L. 10
Berry, J. M. 66–7
Blom, B. 116
Boost, D. 116
Boyne, G. A. 45
Bozeman, B. 14, 16
Brown, T. L. 49–50
Brudney, J. L. 45, 87
Brunton, M. A. 47
Bryson, J. M. 13–16, 126
bureaucratic/bureaucracies 1, 3, 13, 38,
    110
    accountability 31
    service delivery 129
    systems 31

CAAs *see* community action agencies
    (CAAs)
Campbell, D. A. 8–10
Carman, J. G. 9, 11–12
Carnoy, M. 28–9
Chakrabarti, R. 28–9
charitable support, effect of 97
charter school 12, 18, 25, 27, 30
Cheng, Daniel 20, 91
citizens 136
    participation 134
    producers 2
City Parks Alliance 86–7
city park systems 85, 95–7
    acreage of 91
    creation and maintenance of 87
    performance of 86, 89–92, 96
    public outputs of 91
civic capacity 17, 97, 126, 129, 131, 136
civic education 131
civic learning 136
    instances of 16–17
civic participation 67, 135

civil society 112, 126
Coase, W. 47–8
co-design 88, 130
co-determination 10–11
co-finance 88, 130
Cohen, S. 70–71, 89
collaborative environmental management
    69–70
collaborative governance of HIV health
    services 47
collaborative management 46
collaborative networking 68–70, 78
collaborative public management 1
co-maintain 88, 130
co-manage 88, 130
communication 31, 132–3
community action agencies (CAAs)
    19, 64–5, 67, 70, 73, 75–6, 78,
    129–30
    collaborative networking 68–70
    community engagement 67–8, 75
    community sustainability 19, 65–7,
        70, 78
    context of 64
    data and methodological approach
        71–2
        dependent variable 72
        descriptive statistics and
            variable measures 74
        independent variables 72–3
        organizational attributes 73–5
    degree of autonomy 130
    dependence on 64, 70
    effectiveness in community
        sustainability 79
    human resource capacity 68
    implementation of sustainability
        initiatives 129–30
    implications 78–80
    leaders 78
    managers 67, 75, 77
    organizational efficiency 78
    programs 72
    revenue diversification 71
    study results and new insights 75–8
community-based nonprofits 134
community-based organizations 79
community engagement 67–8, 73, 79–80
community resource index 95

Community Services Block Grant
    (CSBG) 71
community sustainability 19, 64–70, 75,
    78
    effectiveness 72
    efforts 75–6
    initiatives 130
    organizational factors on 75–6
    outcomes 66–7
    performance 71, 75–9
    process 68–9
community well-being 16
competitiveness 66
compliance 32, 87, 107, 113, 115, 119,
    133
contemporary public administration 1
content analysis, interpretive approach
    to 110
contracting 56–60
    activities and outcomes 45–7
    implications of 43–4
    public sector 43–4
    for services 49
    theories of 43
contracting out 19, 43–4, 46–7, 54, 56,
    58, 98
Cools, P. 20–21, 131, 135
co-production 2, 87, 89, 125, 130
    individual 87–8
    of local residents 88
    of public services 89
    theory 86, 88–90
    of urban parks 88
corporate ecological responsiveness 66
Corrigan, P. 10
County Health Rankings and Roadmaps
    (CHRR) 19, 44, 53
covenants 105, 112, 115, 117
Cowen, J. M. 29
Cox regression method 35
creative programming 3
Cuttler, Z. 66

data collection 98, 115, 133
decentralization 1, 31–2, 125
decision-making process 67–8, 78, 130
De Corte, J. 105
decoupling 107–9, 118–19
deflection, strategies of 119
degree of legitimacy 3

DeLeon, L. 32
Demsetz, H. 48–9
dependency 69, 73, 108, 115
design effective policy 125
Dias, J. J. , 12
Dickinson, H. 47
Dillman, D. A. 71
diversity of multiple constituents 108
donors 6, 132, 136, 138
Dubnick, M. J. 31

Ebrahim, A. 120–21
Eckerd, A. 126, 130
ecosystem interdependence 67
educational attainment 68
ELIO 104, 110, 112, 115, 119–20
    active doubters 114
    APRVs of 116
    associations of 113
    case study of 119
    choice of 115
    coordinators of 105, 113, 116–18
    financial dependency of 114–15
    network on performance
        measurement 115–17
    poverty and coordinators of 116
    professionals and participants 112
    provisional success 120
    representatives of 112
    respondents of 116
    strategy 117
England, R. E. 87
entrepreneurial civil society 112
environmental dependency 69
environmental responsibility 66
equity 15, 20, 27, 46, 66, 97–8, 134, 137
evaluation criteria 5–6, 8, 12, 79, 117–20
evidence-based medicine 102–3
evidence-based practice 116, 121

fee-for-service contracts 2, 17–18
financial resources 3, 85–6
Fiscally Standardized Cities (FiSCs)
    database 90
Flanders, W. D. 29, 33
flexibility 3, 59, 77, 134
focus groups 103, 109
    with APRV participants 109–10
    with social workers 109–10

Ford, M. R. 18, 29, 32–3, 127, 133
foundations 4, 7, 9, 132, 137
Fredericks, K. A. 9, 11–12
Frederickson, D. G. 3
Frederickson, H. G. 3, 31–2
freedom of choice 127
Friedman, M. 28
"friends of the parks" programs 86, 130
fundraising campaigns 86

Galloway, C. 47
Gazley, B. 10
generational poor 104–5
Giles-Corti, B. 89–90
Glasby, J. 47
Globerman, S. 49
governance 1, 31–2
    fragmentation in urban education
        27–8
    hybrid 1, 27
    network 30
    participatory 134
    public value 14–15
    urban school 30
"governance by distance" approach 106
governance-by-performance approach
    105
government 125
    capacity to deliver services 2
    disinvestment 132
    funding 3
    "good" performance of 126
    institutions 67–8
    and NPOs 105
    partnerships 126
    reliance on nonprofits 2
    role in delivering public services 1
government funding/funders 73, 132,
    134, 137
    consequence of 133
    dependence on 70
    on nonprofit behavior 134–5
Government Performance and Results
    Act (GPRA) 3
Greene, J. P. 28–9
Greiling, D. 105
group co-production 87–8
group production 88

halo effect, reliance on nonprofits 2
Hardina, D. 67
Harnik, P. 86
health outcomes 43–5, 47, 49–50, 53–7
Herfindahl–Hirschman Index (HHI) 73
Hodge, G. A. 45
hollow state
    accountability in 98
    arrangements 13
    assessment of performance in 17
    concept of 17
    description of 1
    governance systems 39
    performance of 17, 98, 125
    public values in 14–17
    urban 78
Housing and Urban Development agency
    (HUD) 9
Hoxby, C. M. 28–9
human resource capacity 73–6
hybrid governance 1
hybrid urban school governance 27–8
hypothesized relationships 49

individual co-production 87–8
individual expression 16, 40, 97, 127–9
institutional demands 107, 113–14
institutional funders 4, 11, 133, 135–6
institutional pressure 106–7
inter-agency collaboration 69
internal performance measurement
    programs 6–7
International Day of Eradication of
    Poverty 131
interorganizational relationships 69

Johnston, J. 45–6
Jolles, M. P. 10

Kalambokidis, L. 13
K-12 education systems 17, 26–8
Koontz, T. M. 69

Lambright, K. 8–9
Langer, J. 9–10
legitimacy 3, 66–7, 69–70, 77, 108, 118
LeRoux, K. 9–12, 18–19, 46, 129
LHDs *see* local public health
    departments (LHDs)

local public health departments (LHDs)
    18, 43–4, 47
    activities of contracting 50
    contract/contractor 55, 58
    impact of 56
    percentage of services 54
    service range 52
local public services 17, 85
logistic regression models 35–6
Lyon, F. 106–8

MacIndoe, H. 6–7
Madden, K. 88
marginalized groups 58, 133
Marsh, R. H. 28–9
Martin, A. 86
math proficiency 18, 35, 37, 127
maximum feasible participation 129–30
Mayer, N. 67
Maynard-Moody, S. 12
*Measuring the Performance of the
    Hollow State* (Frederickson and
    Frederickson) 3
meetings, observation during 111
Meier, K. J. 45–6
Milward, H. B. 1–2, 17, 25, 32, 135
Milwaukee
    education 32, 38
    pupils, distribution of publicly
        funded 30
    school
        public 29
        sectors 29
        voucher policy 29
    voucher experience 30, 39
Milwaukee Parental Choice Program
    (MPCP) 25, 28–9
    accountability framework 38
    education infrastructure 29
    government failure theory 39
    quality control in 30
    research consensus on 29
    schools 29, 32–3
    state accountability 38–9
Milwaukee Public School system (MPS)
    26
    public school 29–30
    student enrollment in 28
Mitchell, G. E. 72
Moody, M. 6

Moore, M. H. 13–14
Morén, S. 116
Morley, E. 11
Moulton, S. 16, 126, 130
MPCP *see* Milwaukee Parental Choice
    Program (MPCP)
multi-sector collaboration 2

National Association of County and City
    Health Officials (NACCHO) 50
National Center on Charitable Statistics
    (NCCS) Core PC files 90
National Recreation and Park
    Association (NRPA) 92
National Taxonomy of Exempt Entities
    (NTEE) codes 91
negotiation, process of 15
new public management (NPM) 14–15,
    102
    reforms 3–4
    theories of 31
    values 3–4
nongovernmental organization 64–5, 69
non-profit organizations (NPOs) 39,
    67–9, 86, 102, 105, 108–9, 112,
    114, 119–20
    anti-poverty 112
    autonomy 113–14
    charitable support for urban parks
        89–90
    context of 103
    data and methodological approach
        90, 93
        analytical approachs 94
        control variables 92–3
        outcome variables 90–91
        predictor variable 91–2
    descriptive statistics for model
        variables 94
    government relations 105, 120
    implications 96–8
    insights for 118–19
    network of 102–3
    parks and recreation 86–7
    performance of 4, 89–90, 102–3
    practices of 116
    relationships 106
    service-providing 120–21
    stakeholders of 108
    strategic responses 106–7

study results and insights 94–6
urban park systems 89–90
nonprofits 2, 5–6, 136
    accountability and performance of
        126
    assessing impact for 6
    capture of 133
    challenges for 132–5
    clients 10–11
    community sustainability by 66
    financial incentives to 12–13
    financial vulnerability of 71
    managers 132, 137
    performance 4–8, 11–13, 16–17, 67,
        132, 134–5
    with program designs 136
    in public service delivery 133
    and public value creation 13–14
        in hollow state 14–16
        specific, identifiable content of
            16–17
    resource scarcity for 134
    school 18, 25, 40, 127
    sector, performance of 4
    service-providing 133–4
    unintended consequences for 134
Norman, R. 114
NPM *see* new public management
    (NPM)
NPOs *see* non-profit organizations
    (NPOs)

Oliver, C. 103, 107, 114–15, 119–20
OLS *see* ordinary least squares (OLS)
ordinary least squares (OLS) 55
    model 94
    regression 75, 94
organizational/organization
    capacity 68–9
    effectiveness 70
    efficiency 76
    leaders 9, 78
    learning 121
    legitimacy 67, 69
    performance 9–10
    publicness 13
    size 73–4
Ostrom, E. 88
O'Toole, L. J. 26, 45–6
outsourcing 45–7, 49, 53, 55, 58–60

Pache, A. -C. 107, 113, 120
parks
    charitable support for 91–2
    conservancies 86
    organization and actual management
        of 88
    public access to 94–5
    public spending on 92, 97
    and recreation services 86
    supporting charities 91–2
    user of 90
Parks, R. B. 88
park-supporting charities 87–8, 91–9,
    130
park system 98
    future research 98
    performance of 94, 96
participatory governance 134
partnership theory 70
Payne, L. L. 92
performance 103–4, 135
    accountability 40
    approach to evaluating 132
    assessment 116
    consequences 3
    data 3
    defining and measuring 4–5
    evaluating 5–8, 127–8
    expectations 134–5
    goals and benchmarks of 113
    holistic view of 135
    implementation of 119
    of nonprofits 4, 8–11, 126
    paradox 12
    perversity 12
    reporting requirements 132
    standards in post-corporatist welfare
        states 105–6
    systems 5, 108–9
    traditional measures of 127, 129
performance measurement 4, 103,
    109–10, 118, 133
    capacity 7
    controversies of 110
    demand for 114, 121
    implementation of 118, 131
    institutional demand for 119
    instruments 121
    method for 112
    systems 108–9

tools 135
Pestoff, V. 2
Peterman, W. 67
Peters, B. G. 31
philanthropic foundations 20, 24, 46
Pierre, J. 31
policy advocacy capacities 134
policy domains 4
policymakers 2, 40
policymaking process 66
Portney, K. E. 66–7
post-corporatist government 106
post-corporatist welfare states 105–6
Potoski, M. 49–50
poverty 20–21, 102–5, 120
    acceptance and avoidance, strategies
        of 107
    controversies regarding pressure to
        measure performance 112–14
    data and methodological approach
        109–11
    implications 120–21
    policy context 104–6
    (pro)active resistance, strategies of
        107–9
    professionals and people in 115
    reduction 118
    risk of 131
    social professional and participants
        in 103
    strategic responses 106–7, 114–20
pregnancy prevention services 56
principal–agent relationship 135
principal–steward model 135
private charitable donations 87
private citizens 4
private nonprofit foundations 20
private organizations 66
proactive decoupling 107–8
(pro)active resistance 107–9
procurement process 16
professional autonomy 107–8
Provan, K. 1–2, 17, 25, 32, 135
public agencies 102
public bureaucracies 2–3
public education 4, 25–6, 29, 127
    compulsory nature of 26
    data and methodological approach
        34–5
    free-market approach to 28

implications 38–40
policy context 26–8
study results and new insights 35–8
voucher policy in Milwaukee 28–31
public funding/funds 2, 28, 70, 87
public health care 4, 117, 129
public health contractors 59
public health services 43, 50
    data and methodological approach
        50–53
        dependent variables 53–4
        descriptive statistics 55
        independent variables 54–5
    implications 58–60
    policy context 43–5
        asset specificity 48
        collaboration and effectiveness
            46–7
        contracting activities and
            outcomes 45–6
        higher transaction cost services
            49–50
        hypothesized relationships 49
        lower transaction cost services
            50
        service measurability 48–9
        transaction costs and
            outsourcing outcomes
            47–8
    relationship 57
    study results and new insights 55–7
public interest theory 13
public libraries 20
public management, consequences for 1
public managers 14, 40, 49–50, 56, 126,
    137
publicness 16, 134
public organizations 3, 130, 136
public parks 86–7, 130
    development and planning for 86
    financing and creating 86
    organizations supporting 88
    private funding and performance
        of 20
    and recreation 4
public–private partnerships 69
public procurement managers 59
public schools 20, 46
public sector ethic 15
public services 132

delivery 31, 46, 125
design and delivery of 89
functions 90
market 43
performance of 85–6, 92
production and delivery of 21
provision of 3–4, 85, 87, 89
quantity of 85–6
types of 105–6
public social welfare services 4
public value 125–6
    accounting 14
    challenges for nonprofits 132–5
    for citizens 2
    conception of 13
    creation 14, 16, 21, 125–6, 132, 135
    expression of 126, 134
    governance 14–15
    government, foundations, and
        citizen donors 135–7
    holistic view of performance in
        hollow state 126–32
    specific, identifiable content of 126
    types of 126

racial diversity 95
Raeymaeckers, P. 20–21, 131, 135
randomized control trials (RCTs) 5–6
realized publicness 16
Reames, T. G. 19, 136
Reames, Tony G. 129–32
recreation services
    charitable support for 91–2
    parks and 86
recreation systems 86–7, 90–91
regular producers 2
reliance
    on government funding 133
    on traditional outcomes 132
religious schools 28, 127
residential weatherization 19, 64, 129
resource dependency theory 69, 108
revenue diversification 19, 71, 77, 80,
    132
revenue diversity 130
Robert Wood Johnson Foundation 53
Rohrer, J. 47
Romzek, B. S. 31, 45–6
Roth, K. 66

Salamon, L. M. 2, 70
Santos. , F. 107, 113, 120
Savas, E. S. 45
schools 127
    choice 18, 25, 30, 136
    lower-performing 18, 25–6
    multinomial logit predicting 37
    survival analysis 35–6
self-confidence 112–13
self-interests 48, 107
self-sufficiency 12, 113, 117–18, 131
semi-structured interviews with
        professionals 109
service delivery 1–3
    collaboration 69
    outcomes of 3
    partners 4
service measurability 48–52
service providers 105
    expectations on 135
service-providing nonprofits 133–4
sexually transmitted infections (STIs)
        33–4, 53–4
Sinclair, A. 47
smoking ordinances 19
social capital 3, 131, 134
social diversity index 92
social impact measurement 109
social innovation 3
social isolation, risk of 104–5
social legitimacy 108
social return on investment (SROI) 6
social services 117
    by non-profit organizations 102
    organizations 20–21
social workers 103, 116, 120
stakeholder groups 8–9
Stoker, G. 15–16
Stötzer, S. 105
strategic behavior, types of 107
strategic management 65, 67, 70, 79
strategic responses 107
sustainability 66, 68, 129
    concept of 64–5
    implementation of 66, 129
    importance of 66–7
    organizational success in 68
    policies 69
    scholars 69

Sustainable Communities Survey 2015
        71
sustainable community, definition of 66
sustainable development 64, 73, 76–9
systemic poverty 129

Texas Assessment of Academic Skills
        (TAAS) 46
Thomson, D. E. 7
transaction costs 44, 47–8, 129
    degree of 19
    lower and higher 53
    outsourcing services 47–8, 50
    theoretical perspectives of 19
    valid measures of 50
trusted messengers 58

United States (US) 25, 64
    American Community Survey
        (ACS) 90
    city park systems in 85–6
    federal government spending 1–2
    public health system 44
    sustainability implementation 70
University of Wisconsin Population
        Health Institute 53
urban development 67
urban education 26
    governance fragmentation in 27–8
Urban Institutes' Outcomes Indicator
        Project 6
urban park systems 86–7, 89–90
    charitable support for 88
    co-production of 88
    performance of 89–90
    private funding for 86
    public investment in 86
urban public education, wicked problem
        of 18
urban public parks 89–90
urban schools
    governance 30
    systems 27
    voucher programs 25
urban society, microcosm of 26
urban sustainability 4
US *see* United States (US)

value creation 14

Vamstad, J. 89
Van der Wal, Z. 13
Van Dooren, W. 32
Van Slyke, D. M. 106–7, 135
variance inflator factor (VIF) 94
Verschuere, B. 105
VIF *see* variance inflator factor (VIF)
Vining, A. R. 49
voluntary failure 70
vouchers 40, 127
   policy in Milwaukee 28–31
   program 18, 25, 27, 33, 38, 127

Walls, M. M. 86–7
WCED *see* World Commission on
   Environment and Development
   (WCED)

welfare states 105–6
Whitaker, G. P. 32
Whitford, A. 47
wicked problems 26–8, 30, 38, 47, 125
   of education 27
Willems, T. 32
Williamson, O. 49
Wisconsin Knowledge and Concepts
   Exam (WKCE) 34
World Commission on Environment and
   Development (WCED) 65–6
Wright, N. 9, 11–12, 19, 129–32, 136

Yu Shi 20

Zhao, T. 18–19, 129